LOvE

The Ultimate Freedom

A World Powerlifting
Champion's extraordinary
shift from physical strength
to a far greater power

ROSIE-MARIA LOVE

First published in 2024 by Wrate's Publishing

Copyright © 2024 by Rosie-Maria Love

Typeset by www.wrateseditingservices.co.uk

A CIP catalogue record for this book is available from the British Library.

Love = Miracles

This is the greatest equation we will ever discover. It is the answer to all life's mysteries and suffering. And it's available to everyone – right here, right now, *if* it is genuinely sought. It *can* be mastered, and it WILL set YOU free!

∼

ULTIMATE LOVE IS FOR-GIVING

When I judge you, I am judging myself.
When I love you, I am loving myself.
When I put pressure on you, I am in fear.
When I get angry with you, I cannot hear.
When I am mean to you, I am in pain.
When I get serious with you, I have forgotten to
*   laugh.*
When I analyse you, I forget I know nothing.
When I try and change you, I am resisting
*   what is.*
When I am resisting what is, I am questioning
*   God.*
When I am unable to hear you, I am not present.
When I am not present, I can't be your gift.
When I need something from you, I am empty.
When I give to you unconditionally, I am full.
And when I am full, I am FOR-GIVING.
By Rosie-Maria Love

A Brief Note on 'God'

As you read through the following events from my life, let me suggest that anyone feeling resistance to the word 'God' simply replace it with the word 'Love'.

Contents

Introduction

My intention for writing this book is to give people hope that we can change.

I once sought love, safety and approval only from the world outside me. Through many profound, lived experiences, I've come to a deep knowing that I am already loved, safe and approved by the Source that created me, and that everything unfolds perfectly. I've never made a mistake because everything is simply an opportunity for growth. As I learned to forgive myself with deep compassion for regrets I once held, I was able to experience deeper compassion for *all* brothers and sisters on this planet. This brought me the peace and happiness I'd been searching for.

I'm not at peace all the time. I still experience those growth opportunities and must remember to put all I've learnt into practice. But I find it gets easier now to bring myself back to Love's answers. And I know if I'm not in peace, my thinking needs to be corrected. After all, it's not the events in our lives that cause us pain, but the way we choose to respond to them.

Every story you're about to read contains the essence of choosing Love over fear. This choice produces profound, life-affirming outcomes, which I liken to miracles.

When we change our perception from fear to Love the unexpected occurs. Often it comes about through forgiveness of oneself, another or a situation. Miracles happen when we totally surrender – we reach a point where our wilfulness to try and control situations becomes useless, and we cry out to God (whether we're religious or not).

My desire is that these true accounts I share with you about my life could help prove to you the power that comes from choosing Love over fear. Miracles can occur if we don't choose to listen to our ego, which reacts and judges. We can learn to trust that, when we ask for something that's greater than the small ego part of our mind, we'll discover a loving way to respond instead. This greater mind, or Source, is referred to by many names, depending on our beliefs: God, Holy Spirit, Higher Power, Higher Self, Buddha, Great Spirit, The Universe, Source, Nature ... It really doesn't matter what we call it. What *is* important is our intention to ask to be a force of Love in action and to not react from ego.

Just asking to be shown the loving answer stops us acting from self-seeking motives. If we don't pause when we're triggered, we'll usually act in self-defence and not be able to see (or even want to see) what's going on for others in a situation. The result is usually more drama, and a lot more heartache, because we're not aware there's another way. These true stories from my life show the result of Love in action and the wonderful results that occur when choosing Love over fear.

When you face your fears and choose Love, you're healing the world. This is the power we have because we *are* all connected. Our thoughts send out signals and affect the world. Thoughts of judgements and fear create illusions that we have enemies, but when we choose loving thoughts, we start to experience a different reality. The 'us versus them' syndrome is dissolved. Instead, daily, we start to reach out to others in the simplest of ways. From Love we can offer a kind word to a stranger or give someone a call just to brighten their day. We can start to see everyone as part of one big family.

When we choose to meet our own internal environment with Love, we overcome our own fears, and it *will* change how we experience the world. When we decide to choose to connect with the Divine Love that we truly are, everything *must* shift. Love will return to each of our lives and eventually, one by one, we *will* change the world. Love will become the dominant force on this planet and we as individuals will bring heaven to earth.

It's so important we know we are *not* here to put all our energy into changing what's outside us. We're not here to change others, or even to try and fix others, but instead to *make this internal shift from fear to Love within ourselves*. A friend of mine recently shared with me that her 85-year-old mother, who was very driven to succeed professionally all her life, looked out the window one day and said, 'None of that out there matters.' With hand on heart, she continued: 'All that matters is what's in my heart!' She was finally at peace.

I want to make this book accessible to those who consider themselves religious, as well as those who do not. When I use the word 'God', which I do many times throughout this book, it's because I have no personal issue with using that word to describe who and what it is I ask guidance from. I'm also comfortable with all the other words used for God, as I feel it's our *intention* that's most important when connecting and asking. *What* we ask for is also very important, so my prayers are always asking how I can respond from Love and not fear.

I often ask simply, 'Please, God, help me to see things differently.' I don't consider myself religious, and I don't feel that 'God' is only used by religious people anymore. I often feel that I'm also speaking to my higher Self when I ask for guidance because I know my soul is the aspect of me that remembers the Truth of who I am. When I lose sight of this – believing I'm *only* this physical body–I experience suffering. I've discovered through my life experiences that when I *do* forget the truth, I can ask God, or my higher Self, for answers … and I'm always heard.

I wasn't brought up to be religious (even though my father's parents were dedicated to Salvation Army). My father's experience was not a pleasant one, so he decided not to follow any religion, but always said he believed that Jesus existed, and He came here to teach us how to be the presence of Love. Growing up, I always felt an affinity with Jesus even though we never went to church or studied the Bible. I always felt I knew Him and that he was somehow close to me, but I never discussed this with anyone. I therefore often speak or pray to Jesus directly when I'm asking for Love's solution.

I always feel I've received the loving answers I've been asking for that I can't access myself. I refer to Jesus as my guide and friend in spirit. Sometimes I'll refer to him in this book as Yeshua, which was his original, Aramaic birth name.

The most important revelation I've received through some of the painful experiences I share is that it's important to be humble enough to ask for help from something greater than our own thinking mind. At first it may be a physical person we consider wiser than us, but eventually, we come to know the real shift that occurs when we're willing to connect to a loving, powerful Source that's always present and waiting to guide us. After all, why is it that so many people who don't believe in a Power greater than themselves cry out to God in their greatest times of despair? It's like there's an inner knowing that never truly leaves us.

Jesus said, 'The Truth will set you free', but what is Truth? One person's 'truth' is often different from another's. But our own ideas of 'truth' are *not* what he was referring to. Wars are justified in the name of religion over different beliefs about what 'truth' is. Most religions primarily began teaching Love, and then the teachings got distorted by the human ego! The truth is so often completely lost; instead, we experience fear and separation. Therefore, it feels very important to understand the meaning of the words 'Love will set you free' and 'The truth will set you free', as I refer to them many times in this book.

So many of us see these phrases as religious and think we must be Christian to experience freedom. 'Free' here means 'free from suffering'. When we choose Love, we find peace instead of confusion and pain. Truth is always based on Love. Unless we're seeking for the loving solution for *all* concerned, we'll keep listening and acting from ego. Our egoic thinking mind wants to control everything to get its own way. The acronym for ego is said to mean 'edging God out'. If God and Love are one and the same, then our egoic thinking mind pushes Love away.

When we feel separate from Love, we remain in a state of victimhood, blame and separation, whereas Love reconnects us to each other and sets us free. So, Love *is* the Truth we've been seeking. Love and Truth are one and the same. When we sincerely pray to God asking for help, what we're asking for is the Truth of God ... and God is unconditional love. God, Truth and Love are interchangeable. I hope to shine a light on this phenomenon by sharing the many miracles I've experienced when I chose Love instead of ego and how this choice freed me from suffering.

What if our journey here on earth is to return to Love? What if our suffering only exists because we've lost touch with what, and who, we really are? It seems that only when we've suffered enough do we even consider being and acting from our true divine nature, which is Love. I feel in my heart that when Jesus said we're made in the image and likeness of God that he was talking about our loving essence.

I hope by the end of this book you may know (as I know) that Love is the most powerful gift we have. That Love is what we are. When we tap into that Love, miracles occur. Love brings miracles that can take us from one dimension to another, and sometimes that shift is so powerful you may never be the same again. Seeing situations and others through the eyes of Love and gratitude, over and over again, will change your whole world and experience here on earth, just as it's changing mine. For most of us it happens gradually over time as we work through all the areas of our lives where judgement and unworthiness are present.

I believe that the opposite of Love is fear. For me, all fear stems from feeling unworthy and unloved. When we truly know we are loved unconditionally by our Creator, there's no need to fear anything. When we know that we are eternal beings of pure Love, and choose to *act* from that Love, we *will* know Truth.

For Love IS Truth, and Love WILL set you free!

Chapter 1

Adopting Negative Beliefs and Fears

For you to truly understand what led me to become so disconnected from Love, adopt negative beliefs, and engage destructive thoughts and fears, it feels important to share some of my childhood experiences. I believe I was simply an innocent child who went to the mind and *created* distorted coping mechanisms to deal with fearful, hurtful situations. But over the years, I came to really identify with my negative thinking patterns.

I feel we *all* are searching for love and safety in the world. As innocent children, we form detrimental strategies to try to survive and avoid feelings of fear.

It usually takes a life crisis for us to become willing to uncover the patterns driving us that ultimately failed to bring us the peace and happiness that they'd been intended to create. After all, how could they have *ever* worked when they came from fear in the first place?

My First Year

When I was born, my mother decided to foster a child. She felt that while she was home looking after me, she could also take care of another baby who needed some love. My parents then chose to take on short-term fostering, so I grew up sharing my parents and home with many children. I believe my parents fostered about 32 children in total. I also had one biological sister who came along three-and-a-half years after I was born. I don't remember much about the early years of my life, but I do remember many foster brothers and sisters coming and going, as well as our home being an open house to all my friends. I feel it was a gift my parents gave me; I now find it so natural to share my home with others. It also prepared me for community living, which is how I now want to live.

I was the first born, and my father spent all his time with me after work. He was always trying to get me on my feet, even shortly after I was born. I think he would've liked me to have been in the *Guinness Book of World Records* for being the youngest baby ever to walk. Even as young as a few months old, I wanted to please my father by responding positively to him. Due to my people-pleasing personality, I walked by myself at seven months old! He was delighted; I got so much recognition and praise from almost everyone who saw me walking at such a young age. I believe this is when, and how, I formed a deep belief pattern that if I achieved and did what others wanted, I would get all the love and approval I needed to stay safe – especially from my parents.

I also know now this is why for so long I felt if I did *not* achieve or stand out by being exceptional at something, I wouldn't be seen. And this would mean I'd be unworthy of love and end up all alone.

Starting School Young

With this achievement belief pattern already running me, I was able to read and write by the time I was four. My parents put me into school early (at age four-and-a-half) because I was advanced for my age. I remember quickly feeling very lonely.

I observed how all the other children who brought in sweets (candy) attracted lots of friends. I remember feeling left out because I was the only one who never had any sweets to share. My father was very strict with what we ate so we'd stay extremely healthy. We were never allowed to have hard sweets, only one small bar of chocolate per week. As a child I just thought he was mean, and I felt very deprived. Later in life, I realised it was his way of showing he cared.

My father did almost everything to the extreme. He sent a letter to the head teacher stating I was not allowed desserts at lunch or sweets at break time. One day, a girl in my class brought in a stick of rock (hard candy) from her holiday vacation. It was huge, and a crowd of children gathered around her to marvel at the brightly coloured rock. In my innocence, I thought that if I pretended the rock was mine, I'd attract some friends and no longer be lonely. When break time came, I took it from her desk. I had no intention of eating it or even keeping it. I pretended it was mine to get some friends, fully intending to return it to her desk afterwards.

I immediately attracted a crowd of children around me, all now *appearing* to be my friends. Of course, the girl who owned the stick of rock went to the teacher to tell her what I'd done. I didn't get a chance to put it back as I was immediately summoned to the office of the head mistress. She'd already informed my parents of what I'd done.

As a child of only four years old, I was terrified. Full of fear, I was unable to speak and communicate my intentions. I don't think I was even asked *why* I did it. They just assumed I stole it to keep it. Both my parents and the teacher told me I was lucky they weren't going to inform the police because they'd arrest me and take me away forever. My parents, who were totally humiliated by my behaviour, threatened to involve the police if I ever did it again.

Parents have no idea what they're doing when they frighten their children into compliance. Mine continued to tell me what a bad girl I was, and my father told me how much shame I'd brought to the family. Their humiliation was so big it stopped them from realising I was only four, and perhaps there was another reason why I took it. Their own fear made them blind. I remember my father was so furious because the head teacher insinuated he was being too strict with me about food. With his anger and the threat of the police, I thought I was going to die. The fear created a belief in me that if I made another mistake, I might never see my parents again. This made me doubt myself and any of my own ideas.

At the time, my parents were everything to me. I didn't

know what to do or think, and I remember feeling like I must never trust myself again to make any decisions without checking with them first. Consequently, I went through the rest of my life needing my parent's approval for almost everything. This need for permission also rolled over into my intimate relationships, and sometimes my close friendships, because of my fear of losing them through a bad decision. If I didn't get approval from those I loved, I found it almost impossible to do something just because I wanted to.

Until the rock incident, my parents had idolised me, but everything changed for me that day. My father was so angry about the whole thing that he took me out of school immediately, and I had to go to another school that was much farther from where we lived. I was blamed for the rest of my childhood for why my sister and I had to go to the other school, which was a much longer walk.

I was called a thief, in a teasing way, by my parents and siblings for years afterwards. So, at only four years old, I took on the belief I was bad and couldn't trust myself. I also felt I wasn't enough just being me, so in order to make friends I believed I had to buy them in some way or be who *they* wanted me to be, and not who *I* wanted to be. This experience has shown me how important it is to make our children feel safe enough to explain their actions rather than just assuming they're 'bad'. Instilling fear in our children to try and prevent them from doing something has devastating effects.

Physical Trauma at a Young Age

At age three-and-a-half, I experienced my first major physical and mental trauma.

My mother, talking to a friend, had left me and my siblings on the other side of the road from her. I was eating crisps and wanted to offer some to my mother. As I ran into the road, I was struck by a car. My mother turned around in time to see my little body flying through the air. She says she fell to her knees in devastation, whilst eight months pregnant with my younger sister. When she finally got to my body, blood was coming from my mouth. She was sure I was dead. The ambulance arrived quickly but as I was being moved, I let out a terrifying scream. Although horrific for my mother to see me in so much pain, she felt relieved I was at least alive.

I had broken my left femur bone and badly bitten my tongue. Apart from this, I didn't have a bruise or scratch! But I was in a great deal of physical pain. The femur bone needed to be realigned. A process called traction (which is now rarely used) was applied, which involved stretching the bone upward to heal the break. They strapped both my legs into a vertical position, telling my family it would take six weeks of lying like this to fully heal.

Family members tell me now how disturbing it was to visit me in the hospital, as it was full of children screaming for their parents ... including me. Back in those days, parents weren't allowed to visit their kids anytime they wanted (only at lunchtime and in the evening), so children were left alone for long periods of time. I remember being talked to sternly by a nurse just for crying for my mother! I'd make my family members leave something with me, like their watch, so I could make sure they'd come back from using the toilet. I also felt self-conscious that I wasn't allowed to wear a nappy or knickers and so was very exposed from the waist down. Despite that, I'd cry and beg my family not to leave when visiting hours were over.

Those weeks in the hospital were long and terrifying. I was separated from my parents for the first time, and constantly surrounded by cries and screams from other children. A two-year-old boy who'd fallen into a bath full of boiling water lay in the bed next to mine. Even my mother said she had a difficult time seeing him so badly disfigured. I was in pain myself, alone, scared, and being told by nurses that I was naughty for crying. I realize now how very traumatizing this experience was for such a young child!

When I was finally allowed to go home, my mother made clear that I must always listen to her in the future and not be a naughty girl. After all, she'd told me to stay where I was that day, but I hadn't listened, and look what happened! I believe this was the onset of my deep-rooted fear of making mistakes and the horrendous consequences I thought would happen by doing so. It seemed to me that even if my intentions were good, making a mistake was to be deeply feared. One of my life's lessons has been to undo this thinking and be able to make decisions without needing permission from others first.

Sexual Abuse by My Grandfather

Like most grandparents, mine had the time to spend with me that my parents didn't always have. They lived only five doors away from where we grew up. I loved both my grandmother and grandfather. I'd spend most evenings and weekends with them to escape the drama at home. With two parents who were heavy drinkers, there was always something going on, and I wanted to get away from it all.

I particularly loved having dinner with my grandparents and watching TV with them. I'd get to eat chocolate and desserts without my parents knowing, as my grandmother thought my father was far too strict with us about sweet food. If mum came in unexpectedly, we'd hide what we were eating under the sofa so we wouldn't get in trouble.

I also loved the fact that my grandfather spent so much one-on-one time with me. He was like my best male friend. We'd play darts in his shed, and he'd often play the piano and sing to me. My grandparents meant the world to me, and I didn't want anything to jeopardise that.

I have very little memory of everything that occurred as I was so young, but I do remember my grandfather touching me inappropriately. Because it felt nice, I didn't know it was wrong. I told my auntie, when I was about five years old, that grandad was rubbing cream on my private parts like it was all perfectly normal. Fifty years later, she said she wished she'd said something at the time, because she intuitively knew something wasn't right.

As I got older, my grandfather would sometimes make me look at magazines of naked women while rubbing himself up against me from behind. Looking back, I believe he remained fully clothed because my nan could have walked in at any time.

One day, when I was around eight years old, I gathered the courage to tell my grandfather that I didn't think we should be doing this. To my horror, he became really angry, almost snarling like a dog while shouting that I didn't know what I was talking about and that we were doing nothing wrong. I distinctly remember a feeling of terror that I'd upset him so much.

Once again, I concluded I could *not* trust my feelings and intuition. The thought of losing my grandfather's love and attention felt like death, so I made myself wrong. I remember thinking that I'd rather put up with this behaviour than lose him. It came to be that I carried this belief into adulthood and put up with a lot of abusive behaviour from loved ones rather than lose them. It wasn't always sexual abuse but abuse in general. This included intimate partners, other family members and even bosses.

The sexual abuse lessened but didn't stop completely until I was 13. My grandfather always called this rubbing up against me 'wrestling'. One day, in my own home, we were watching a program on TV where two people were rubbing themselves up against each other fully clothed in a passionate way. I blurted out that my grandad did this to me, and he called it wrestling. All my father said was that it was *not* wrestling, and that if he tried to do it again, I was to tell him that dad said so. I felt that now I had permission to say something; it wasn't just coming from me. So this is exactly what I said to my grandfather the next time it happened. As soon as I repeated those words, saying they came from my father, he never touched me again.

I didn't mention the abuse to anyone else until I was in a Twelve Step program and had to acknowledge my own shame, guilt and fears surrounding it. I later discovered I wasn't the only one grandfather had abused, although I wouldn't learn this for another forty years.

I have forgiven and healed the shame I carried, and I feel incredibly lucky to have done so. Grandfather died before the abuse was revealed to the rest of the family. I'm convinced he was abused himself as a child.

The Swimming Pool Incident

Growing up, swimming and diving were activities the whole family enjoyed. My father was very adventurous and taught us to have no fear when it came to physicality. I loved that about him. He'd find safe places for us to jump off bridges into rivers, and he always drew a crowd when he performed inward roll bombs and splashed anyone who walked by. He could be very mischievous, and we all loved it!

As a treat in the summer, we started going to outdoor swimming pools. My father would do handstand dives, and teenagers would ask him to teach them how to do it. I loved that he was so well-liked. And although what I'm about to tell you added to my fear of life – and fear of my father – I know my father wasn't a bad person; he just didn't know how to deal with situations that didn't go his way. I know now it was his own fears that he'd never acknowledged or dealt with that produced his over-reactions to events in his life.

From a very young age, even before I could properly swim, I loved it when my father would drop me from the diving boards. He'd literally dangle me over the water and drop me as straight as he could. I wanted him to do this because I didn't have the nerve to actually jump off the diving boards by myself. I'd wear arm bands to help me float, and my father would jump in after me to make sure I got out of the water safely. I was about three or four years old, but I could tell how my father loved my bravery. It also attracted a lot of attention from onlookers: I got to stand out and get noticed, which fed my belief that *this* was how I'd survive in life. (All of this was of course running me unconsciously at the time, but with deep self-honesty in my later life I came to understand my behaviour.)

Eventually, I had the courage to jump off the high boards by myself while still wearing my arm bands. I was about five years old and could swim without them, but when jumping into the water they gave me that extra reassurance that I'd be safe.

One day, there was a new lifeguard on duty who didn't know our family. He was shocked at what he was seeing, so he blew his whistle and told my father I wasn't allowed to jump off the boards unless I could swim without arm bands. My father told him I could indeed swim but wearing them gave me the courage to jump. Still, the lifeguard said he wouldn't allow it unless I proved that I could swim the whole length of the pool. I only managed to swim three-quarters of the full-length swimming pool as my little body just couldn't quite make it. Just before grabbing the side of the pool, I remember fearing my father would no longer love me if I failed.

My father was furious with me – which proved my belief that I would lose love and bad consequences would happen if I didn't achieve a task. (I know now it wasn't that I lost his love, but that he didn't like being seen as wrong.) He was also angry with the lifeguard because, despite my great effort, he still insisted I couldn't jump off the diving boards. The whole family had to leave because my father was so angry.

On the way home in the car, his anger turned to me and he started to blame me for embarrassing him because I didn't try hard enough. He exclaimed we couldn't possibly go back there again as a family, so we'd never return. My brothers and sister became angry with me too, and I got blamed for why our wonderful days out at this open-air pool were no longer going to happen.

Once again, at a very young age, it was *my* fault that we couldn't return to an activity the entire family enjoyed.

A Champion Diver at Age Seven

Life continued and I buried my fears.

We still went swimming outdoors in rivers and canals in the summertime (which was actually more fun.) My family forgot about the swimming pool incident after a couple of years, and by the time I was seven years old I was jumping off the high boards and bridges wherever we went. I'm not sure whether I enjoyed the diving itself or the attention I received for doing it.

My mother, with all good intentions, thought that since I

loved diving so much, perhaps I could get professionally coached. I joined a diving club, and it didn't take long before I was winning competitions and doing dives only boys had previously performed. I became well-known for setting the bar higher for girl divers, and I was regularly featured in the local newspapers for winning almost every competition I entered.

While I felt the need to win to get love, safety and approval from others, I also felt badly for those who came in second or third. I started to dislike the competitive side of diving. My coach was extremely strict, but I grew fond of her anyway. She'd have me train before school and sometimes even take me out of school during lunch breaks. Consequently, I'd eat at a table by myself when I got back, which caused even more separation from the other children.

I felt my coach was becoming too obsessive with all the training, so I'd spend most of my days at school dreading diving sessions in the evenings. My friends would all be gathering to play after school, but of course I couldn't join them. I began to hate my life. I made no long-lasting friends from school because I was always the outsider. I asked my parents if I could stop diving, but because I was winning almost every competition I entered, they wouldn't give me their permission. They used to say, 'You're too young to know what's good for you. You must like it because you're doing so well'! My mother was so proud of me, always talking about my achievements, and my coach wanted me to go to the Olympics. Because of past consequences when I tried to make my own decisions, I was terrified of being wrong again, and so desperately thought I needed my parent's permission to stop diving.

My younger sister had no problem saying 'no' to my parents. I could never understand why she was so confrontational. I used to think she was crazy for not needing their approval for anything. I've since learnt that we were complete opposites in the ways we tried to feel safe in the world. She felt safer and more in control by saying 'no' to almost everything my parents wanted her to do, and I thought I'd find my safety by pleasing them. My need to please others became very detrimental to my actual safety.

I was about twelve years old when I hit my hand on the diving board and broke my little finger performing a reverse dive. It was the day before the national championships, which I was expected to win for my age group. My coach (who was also a nurse) ordered me to stop being a baby, get back on the diving board and perform it again, despite me holding my hand and crying in pain. Through my tears I dove again. As my hand hit the water it bent the finger back. The pain was excruciating.

The following day, I competed and did *not* do well due to the pain I was suffering. After the competition was over, my mother took me to the hospital, where we discovered my finger was broken. Looking back on this, once again it showed my inability to say no to an adult – even when it resulted in extreme physical pain. I didn't trust my own feelings and judgement, and I was also terrified of the repercussions of upsetting my parents and my coach.

Due to my success as a diver, I was constantly in the local newspaper. The attention I received seemed to create even more hostility from children at school. I was ostracised by the popular kids and often felt very lonely and left out, especially at break times. At home, with three foster children older than me and a sister three-and-a-half years younger, I was hardly ever around to bond with them. I once again felt alone, different and disliked by my own siblings. This made it seem even more important for me to achieve well to gain attention from my parents and my coach. I believed they were the only people who cared about me, reinforcing my drive to please them instead of feeling free to be myself and make my own decisions.

Because of this belief, I ended up attracting people who didn't love me for who I was but rather for what I could do. I longed to be loved without needing to prove myself but I had a deep-seated belief that I was not enough just being myself. My belief created my reality. This pattern played out in every aspect of my life.

Living with Alcohol-Dependent Parents

I grew up feeling a lot of fear, but I was very good at not showing it. I kept everything hidden behind a smile. *After all, I thought, no one wants to be around someone who shares with them how miserable they really feel.*

My father, who I desperately wanted approval from, was extremely frightening to me because I never knew what would set off his anger. I tried frantically to get his rules right so he wouldn't shout at me. Unfortunately, it didn't seem to matter what I did most of the time, as so many interactions with him ended with him annoyed with something I did or the way I expressed myself. It was confusing: I knew he really loved me, but I just couldn't feel it because of the way he acted.

Father was a big drinker. When he drank, he was fun and relaxed, but it made him angrier and more agitated the next day. He didn't realize how drinking affected his mood and reactions. My mother, who most of the time drank 'secretly' (believing we didn't know), was often very loud and embarrassing. We could smell the alcohol so strongly coming through her body and breath the next day. It was like they thought if they were happy drunks, then no one was negatively affected. This was a confusing nightmare for us, because one minute they were on our side, but then the next day, they were having a go at us for the same thing they'd agreed with while drunk!

No one could question Mum's drinking, or even insinuate we knew she was drinking too much, as she'd completely deny it. If Mum wasn't loud, we often didn't realise how much she'd drunk, so it was a surprise when she didn't remember things we'd spoken about. She'd regularly forget conversations and arrangements she'd made with us.

One day I paid her back some money I owed her and asked her to write it down on the calendar. She got very cross about me suggesting she write it down, saying she'd definitely not forget. The next day she asked me for the money again. I thought she was having fun with me, so I laughed and said, 'Very funny, Mum'. She looked totally bemused; it became clear she wasn't joking. When I repeated our conversation from the previous day, she viciously called me a liar. Luckily, I remembered where she'd put the money.

I showed her where it was, and when she realised she was wrong, she scowled at me and walked away, never mentioning it again.

I loved my mum, but I also hated her for her behaviour. Due to her drinking, denial was a frequent issue. Living with such denial caused me to doubt myself. Mum would sound so convincing that certain incidents had *not* happened during her blackouts that, over the years, it caused me to doubt my own mind. It was like being gaslighted. I then began to hate myself, my life *and* my parents. I felt overwhelmed by my emotions and often thought suicide was an option. It seemed a sort of comfort to me, because if it all became more than I could handle, it would be a way out of my emotional pain.

I never shared my fears, self-loathing, or any of these negative thoughts with anyone. I kept it all hidden inside.

First Bout of Depression

The first time I experienced depression was around the age of 15. I was studying for my final exams in school and found myself in great turmoil and fear at the thought of failing them. My father was forever telling us that women were basically less than and stupid compared to men, and he often accused me of being like this, too. The thought of failing my exams was terrifying to me, as I'd taken on the belief that I *needed* to succeed to survive. This belief went so deep that the thought of failing felt crucifying. My bout of depression became so unbearable I couldn't keep it to myself; I broke down and told my grandmother.

Grandmother showed me unconditional love. I don't know if my childhood would've been bearable if it wasn't for her love. I shared with her that I felt terrible, that I couldn't stop crying. She held me and told me everything would be alright. That was all I needed to hear. She gave me love, with no judgement.

I went on to pass my exams with high grades (except two, which I retook the following year). Even if I *had* failed them, the love and understanding I received from my grandmother would've gotten me through it all. Sharing my feelings with grandmother, and having them heard, was my first experience of actually feeling *better* after talking things through with someone I could trust. Later in life, I learned how vital it was for my well-being to not hide my problems behind a smile.

The Turning Point

At the age of 35, I was deeply co-dependent with my partner. I needed him to stop drinking and became obsessed with this situation that I ultimately couldn't control. I loved him deeply, but truly believed *he* was the problem.

I became very ill with painful migraines. Eventually I was diagnosed as chronically depressed. My doctor wanted to put me on antidepressants, but I knew how addictive and harmful they could be, so I declined. But I knew something had to change in my life. At that point, I thought ending the relationship was the only way. But after only a month, we got back together, and the headaches returned.

One night, when my partner was very drunk, I told him

I couldn't be with him anymore. He was so angry, he punched the wall and then tried to kill me by putting a pillow over my face. I managed to get him off me by punching him as hard as I could. I grabbed my keys and ran out the door to my sister's. She recommended a Twelve Step program called Al-Anon, for people affected by someone else's drinking. This was a life-changing experience for me – the program's steps were extremely powerful.

The program addressed my co-dependency, and I saw why I allowed myself to stay in dysfunctional relationships. It was the first time I looked at myself and the negative patterns that were running me. I was able to see my distorted perceptions of myself, life and others that caused my depression.

It took a lot of courage, honesty, vulnerability, and humility to reach a point where I could choose Love over fear. It did *not* occur without a lot of self-awareness, which was cultivated over many years. The pain and challenges in my life became the catalyst for growth and healing. My suffering became my gift.

Wanting to end my life enabled me to be open to another way. It was the 'gift of desperation', sometimes referred to as a person's 'rock bottom'. I became open to looking at myself and taking full responsibility for my thoughts and perspectives on life, which I later discovered were definitely the cause of all my suffering.

I'd become lost without my spiritual connection. Applying the steps in this program revealed how I'd allowed myself to be deceived by a false mental mind.

Changing My Perception

I view my upbringing very differently now, compared to when I was growing up.

I see that my parents and grandparents were perfect for me in every way for the life lessons I needed to learn. I no longer blame them for all my shortcomings, because they did the best they could with what they'd learnt from *their* parents. Everything that happened became the catalyst for my own healing later in life. The pain I endured in adulthood was due to my own perspective and reactions to all that'd happened in the past. It was my *own* thoughts and behaviours I had to have the courage to look at to be set free. This enabled me to forgive myself and others.

It also enabled me to see why I was attracting the same unpleasant scenarios. I really want to emphasise that I do *not* blame my parents for how *I* reacted to what happened. I truly believe I came into this life to learn to love myself and others unconditionally, and they were the perfect parents to assist me in this. I always knew my parents really loved me, which was (and still is) a great gift they gave me. Their reactions from their *own* fears obviously had a negative effect on me, but I know it was all a perfect setup for my own healing and growth.

In fact, I learnt to love my mother by choosing to focus on her many gifts: She was always willing to help anyone whenever she could. She loved to cook lovely food for her family and friends; this was her favourite way of showing her love for us. It was her hard-working, giving nature that made it possible for my parents to foster over 30 children during our childhood.

Through my own healing, I was able to stop judging my mother for not being able to deal with her emotions, which caused her to drink. I stopped thinking about myself and realised how hard her life must have been having not dealt with her own childhood traumas. All my resentments changed to huge compassion, which allowed me to love her.

In February 2023, I was with my mother in hospital when she was put on palliative care. Her heart, liver and kidneys were failing. I moved into the family home and looked after her for the last two months of her earthly life. It was the most precious time I'd ever spent with her, and I am so grateful to have witnessed what a beautiful Soul she was (and is). For the 10 months leading up to this time, she'd not been able to drink any alcohol, so I really got to know her sweetness. We laughed and cried and told each other every day how much we loved each other. She never complained once and was constantly thanking everyone for all they were doing for her. This beautiful experience with my mother was only possible because I chose to extend the power of love and forgiveness. I now only feel a loving warmth in my heart for both of my parents, who are each no longer on the planet.

This compassion also helped me forgive myself for the mistakes I made in my own parenting when my sons were young. I'm grateful for *everything* that's occurred. I've learnt that all my suffering has come from my own thinking and fears. This knowing has brought me freedom and a sense of empowerment, as I now know I am *not* a victim of this world. I am, in fact, capable of tuning into higher frequencies –

through joy and truth – that attract very different experiences into my life.

You could say I now create a different reality that is much more delicious and makes life a wonder to behold, instead of one to endure. I've discovered the truth, and:

The Truth Will Set You Free!

Chapter 2

A Healing Miracle with My Father

Have you ever wondered what it would be like if you could tell one (or both) of your parents everything you've ever wanted to say to them but never dared to, both how much you love them *and* the ways they've hurt you? The following story resulted in a healing miracle with my father at a time we thought he was going to die. I was given the opportunity to share with him how much I loved him, as well as all the unspoken resentments I'd swallowed over and over again throughout my life.

I was very close to my father in many ways: We both valued our health and fitness, we shared the same spiritual views, and we could speak together at a deep level on many subjects. We also formed a close bond when I was a baby. I was the firstborn, and apparently, he carried me in his arms everywhere he went, which was particularly interesting because he was against hugging, shaking hands or any form of tactile expressions; my father didn't talk about his feelings at all (and he couldn't stand anyone else talking about their feelings, either). But he adored babies, and young children definitely brought out the softer side of him.

My father's passion was weight training. He ran a weightlifting gym, and it was a huge part of his life. It started out as a small, private gym in a garden shed just for the family, but later developed into a large, public gym. My father kept the fee low, making it accessible for those who couldn't afford the usual rates at the larger gyms. He'd often take young lads under his wing, coaching many of them into becoming weightlifting champions, without charging them a penny for his coaching!

In his gym, he had a rule written on the noticeboard stating, 'Don't ask me how I am'. He couldn't stand being asked to describe how he felt, even with everyday language. I have no idea what happened to him as a child or what messages he received to be so resistant to any form of endearment or expression of feelings. What I did experience, however, was how easy it was for him to hold a newborn and talk to them. He never spoke to them like they were babies, as he never believed in 'all that baby talk'; if he heard anyone talking that way, he'd get angry and put them in their place. But he always jumped at the chance to be with his grandchildren whenever he could and enjoyed them tremendously. He'd tell them funny stories, conversing with them the whole time he was carrying them around – and they loved him!

As I shared in Chapter 1, when I was born, my father was determined to get me walking as soon as possible. I'm not sure why, but as young as only a few weeks old, I responded by wanting to please him. The result was that I walked at only seven months old! This explains the close relationship I had with my father and represents how I wanted to please him by performing well and achieving a lot.

I idolised my father and loved him, so much. I felt I always needed his approval, but at the same time, I was terrified of his anger. It wasn't because I thought he would hit me; he never did. It was the feeling his anger produced in my body when he shouted at me that was so unbearable. Due to my desperate need to please him, it felt like the end of the world each time it happened ... and it happened almost every day, in some form or another. There were times I just wanted to die to get rid of the feelings of incredible fear and hopelessness it produced.

When I was 14 years old, I started weight training. My father was my coach. I'd been a competitive springboard diver for the previous seven years. Even though I'd been a national champion as a diver, I absolutely hated it. One day, I finally managed to convince my parents to allow me to stop diving, telling them I was really miserable. The condition from my father was that I start training with weights to stay fit; he told me, 'You don't want to get fat'. I ended up enjoying the training – and the way it made me look. It also pleased my father immensely, especially when I started winning competitions and breaking British records at a young age.

I became a British powerlifting champion in my weight class by the time I was 15 and attended my first world championship in Hawaii at 16. I was the youngest competitor to lift and felt really pleased to win a third-place medal. It was wonderful to see the delight it brought to my father and to get the chance to travel the world.

When my father was in his sixties, he started having serious heart problems. For many years, he'd had a slight arrhythmia and high blood pressure, but it was only in his late sixties that these issues became a real problem. He had to sleep in a more upright position because he couldn't breathe very well when lying down, so ended up sleeping in a recliner chair in the living room. He couldn't walk more than about 20 steps without becoming breathless. Results from hospital tests showed that one of the valves in his heart was working at only 20 percent capacity. Doctors told him there was nothing they could do for him – it was only a matter of time before a backflow of blood would cause his instant death.

I was devastated. And I couldn't imagine what it must've been like for him to hear this dreadful news. When I saw my father and how disheartened he was, I felt extremely helpless.

At the time, I was hosting weekly gatherings with friends where we studied the book *A Course in Miracles*. A woman from America offered to come to my house and give a talk about a process called The Power of Clearing. She spoke about the many miracle healings she'd witnessed whilst facilitating this work for others, especially those who had serious illnesses and relationship issues. She'd been inspired by *A Course in Miracles* and created this process based on its principals.

After hearing the woman speak, I was inspired! I invited my father to come to one of her talks and (to my surprise) he accepted. While he didn't believe anything could help him at this stage, he was willing to hear what she had to say. After attending her introductory presentation, he was still very despondent and not willing to have a session with her or participate in her course, which started the following day. He felt he was beyond help.

The next day, the woman called me and asked if I was aware that his condition was a life-or-death situation. I told her I was well aware of that, and so was my father. She asked me to tell him how important it was that he do this process, and that he really needed to come to the weekend course she was holding in London, which started that evening.

I thought she was crazy for asking him to go to something that started that same day, knowing how ill he was. I also thought she was pushy and controlling to call me on the telephone after my father had already said 'no' to her. I was sure she had no idea how angry my father would be with me if I even suggested such a thing. The course was going to cost a lot of money and I had a judgement that she was just trying to get more participants. I told her I wasn't happy about calling him and that I wasn't prepared to put myself in a situation where I'd be shouted at by my father for asking him again. Then she said something that interrupted my ego mind and really made me think:

'Take him out of the box you have him in from the past and just ask him.'

I knew what she meant. I was aware of how we can bring the past into the present and act in ways that produce the same results. I realised that, just because my father had acted like that before, it didn't necessarily mean he'd react the same way again. She then added, 'Please tell him I've asked you to call him because it *is* a life-or-death situation.'

So, I took a deep breath and, with my whole body shaking, called him. I repeated exactly what the woman had told me to say. There was a moment of silence. I waited. I wasn't expecting *silence* – I was expecting him to get annoyed straight away. Surprisingly, he replied in a very subdued voice, saying if he could change an appointment he had the next day then perhaps he could go. Not wasting a second, I blurted out, 'If you go, I'll go too.' He replied, 'Okay, I'll see what I can do and call you back in 20 minutes.' I was stunned! I remember standing in my kitchen completely dumbstruck, wondering what on earth had just happened. This in itself felt like a miracle! It was one of those moments when I felt delighted to be wrong. He called me back within ten minutes and said he'd changed his appointment and was able to go. I was so excited, wondering what an amazing opportunity this might bring for both of us.

We had to take a 30-minute train journey followed by a 20-minute walk from the station to the venue. That was when I saw how ill my father actually was; every 20 steps, he'd have to stop and catch his breath. I felt heartbroken as he looked at me with despair. There was a silence in that moment that spoke a thousand words. We continued slowly but eventually arrived. It was such an unbelievable struggle for him to walk that we realised we'd need to get a taxi from the train station the following day.

That first evening, we had to introduce ourselves by telling the group why we were attending the workshop. There were about 40 people present. My father was one of the last to share. When it was his turn, he looked around the room and said, 'Well, basically I'm fucked.' This made everyone laugh and created a relaxed atmosphere. He explained that he didn't really feel anything could help him at this stage, but he had nothing to lose by attending this workshop.

The next day, we returned to discover how this Power of Clearing process worked. We were separated into smaller groups, and I wasn't with my father. A qualified coach facilitated each group. In mine, I was asked what was coming up for me in my life that caused pain or unhappiness. All I could talk about was my father and how much I loved him.

I usually found it hard to cry in front of others, but I was feeling so much pain at the thought of my father dying, I couldn't stop crying. It brought up intense emotion for me knowing that he didn't have that long to live.

I explained how I felt I could never get things right for him and shared that he was always shouting at me. I told them what really made me sad was that I didn't believe he loved me, because he'd never told me so. I was then invited to pick someone from the group to play my father and to share my feelings directly with them as if they actually *were* him, sitting in front of me. In this first stage of the three-stage process, we were learning how to communicate in a way that facilitates healing.

During the lunch break, my coach took me aside and said, 'If you do this work directly with your father, not only will it help *you* heal, but it'll help heal your father too.' I trembled at the thought of being so vulnerable with him. My father would berate us if we cried; he said it was a selfish act. I felt he thought it was a weakness. My father was very proud of the fact he hadn't cried since he was about five years old. I knew I wouldn't be able to stop myself from bursting into tears, as the coach was suggesting I express everything I'd ever wanted to say to my father directly to him, and make eye contact with him as much as possible. I didn't know if I had the courage to tell him *everything*.

I so desperately wanted to tell him how much I loved him, as well as how much I resented him for his anger. Usually, communication with my father consisted of him mostly talking and me listening. I never dared speak about my feelings, especially if it had anything to do with him, and so I was absolutely terrified about any such interaction. I remember watching films with my family and fighting back tears to look good in my father's eyes, while my sister and mother would be sniffling through the whole movie. He would tease them for showing their feelings, which was an added reason for me not to show mine. I remember the tightening pain in my throat and how my chest burned as I held it all in. Yet, here I was, given the chance to express everything to my father, knowing I wouldn't be able to stop myself from crying. I was deeply afraid of his reaction, despite knowing that in *this* process, all he was allowed to say in response to anything I said was, 'Thank you'.

I had an hour to think about what the coach had

suggested. Even though it terrified me, I knew in my heart and soul that I had to go through with it. The thought of going home and losing this opportunity to heal with my father felt dreadful, so I knew it wasn't an option.

After lunch, I agreed to go ahead with the process, and my father was called over. There were four of us in our group – myself, my father, the coach and a fourth person asked to be a loving presence without speaking. The coach was there to make sure the process was carried out properly, and especially to make sure my father only said 'thank you' in response to what I said I thought about him, rather than being defensive. This made me feel a bit safer to share everything I'd ever wanted to express to him.

Despite all that, sitting opposite my father was terrifying. I started to shake noticeably. Speaking those first words felt impossible. I wanted to run but knew I couldn't. I took a deep breath and began.

'Dad, what I want you to know is that when you shout at me, I feel devastated because I just want you to love me'. He replied, 'Thank you.' I could tell it was hard for him not to say more. I continued.

'Dad, what I want you to know is when you get angry with me, I feel such a deep pain in my heart, and I feel that I must repulse you.' Again, he replied with, 'Thank you', but this time I could see the despairing look in his eyes and how uncomfortable it was becoming for him as I shared my true feelings.

At this point, my lip started to quiver, and my eyes filled up with tears. I was trying so hard not to completely fall apart, and my entire body started to shake as I said:

'Dad, I love you so much, but I am terrified of you.'

As the words left my mouth, I completely lost it and broke down in tears. I cried so hard I couldn't keep eye contact anymore as my head dropped into my hands. It was so hard to allow him to fully see me as I cried so uncontrollably. When I managed to look up, through tears and with snot pouring from my nose, I saw my father shaking, his eyes filling up with tears. He looked so helpless. The look on his face reminded me of a lost little boy. He just didn't know what to do with himself or his feelings.

In that moment, I saw him for the first time without a tough exterior; his hard-heartedness was softening. I could see my love for him and his love for me was cracking him open as he became more vulnerable. He desperately wanted to say something in defence, but the coach gently touched his arm and said, 'Just say thank you, Ken.' So, he did.

I continued to share my feelings until I felt I'd expressed to him everything I hadn't had the courage to say before. Finally, that part of the process was complete.

The next part of the healing session continued. Here, I was to discover what I *thought* his anger meant about me and express it verbally to him. I began by saying, 'Dad, forgive me for believing that when you shouted at me, I made it mean that I meant nothing to you.' The words he was given to say at this point were, 'That is a story you made up, and I love you.'

I'd never heard the words *I love you* come from his lips before, so I was wondering how hard this would be for him. But something quite amazing happened. He leaned forward, looking deep into my eyes, and with every part of his being, said, 'That is a story you made up, and I love you.' I lost it again, crying hard as his words started to melt my heart *and* his.

I continued to express the stories I'd made up about myself due to his anger. The more I shared, the more he desperately wanted me to hear him, to the point that he was almost shouting the words, 'That is a story you made up, and I love you!' The last one I remember saying was, 'Forgive me for believing that when you shouted at me, I thought I was worthless and that there was something seriously wrong with me for making you so angry.' Once again, he repeated the words, looking me straight in the eyes, expressing himself with so much love and compassion.

As my father spoke these words over and over again to everything I'd made his anger mean about me, I noticed he was literally changing before my very eyes: His demeanour was softening, and his armour had completely shattered. He looked like a different person from the man who sat before me at the beginning of the process. It was clear that just saying the words 'I love you' over and over again was having a profound effect on him, especially as he was expressing those words with so much emotion and compassion.

In the final part of the process, I got to say to my father, 'Forgive me for forgetting that I am love'. His part was to repeat the words back to me, making direct eye contact so I could fully receive his words. He replied, 'Yes, you are love. That is the truth, and I love you.' The emotion was intense as I cried once more, but this time it was different. I was crying and smiling at the same time, as my tears of joy and relief flowed. A huge weight had been lifted from me by sharing so many years of unspoken feelings. I felt so much love flowing through my heart for myself and for my amazing father who sat before me. I could feel the love emanating towards me from his eyes and body language; it was clear that nothing else mattered to him in that moment but my understanding how much he loved me and for me to accept the truth of who I was!

I continued down the list of truths that were written on a sheet of paper as part of the process – all the qualities of our true essence that we forget when we come to earth. Another powerful truth I'd forgotten was that I'm innocent in the eyes of our Creator, so I proceeded to declare: 'Forgive me for forgetting that I am innocent.' My father continued to reaffirm the truths back to me, followed by the words 'I love you'.

When we were finally complete, I sat on his lap, and we hugged as if we'd just met for the first time. I continued to cry on his shoulder in joy as we hugged each other tightly. When the hug felt complete, my father looked around at everyone with desperation in his eyes and said, 'I had no idea! I had no idea!' He then looked at me and said, 'I have always been so proud of you. I had no idea that you were believing all those things about yourself. I love you, and I have never been more proud of you than I am right now. The courage and the life you are pursuing on your spiritual path I could never do. I want you to know I admire you, and I know what you are doing is right.' Everyone who'd been in the process with us was also crying and beaming with joy as he spoke these words. It was truly an awesome moment.

Afterward, I felt amazing and so unbelievably light!

Freedom and joy filled my being. I no longer had all those unwanted feelings inside me running my life, and I felt the love and connection with my father I'd always longed for. My father was beaming from ear to ear, the happiest I'd ever seen him. He had a sparkle in his eyes that I'd never seen before. The fear, anxiousness and hard shell he exhibited when he first arrived had been shattered. He was laughing and joking around with everyone he spoke to, adding 'and I love you' to almost every sentence he spoke.

I also noticed he didn't seem to be in pain anymore. I said nothing at the time because I didn't want to assume anything. He continued to make us laugh all the way home with his joking around. It was a truly remarkable journey that I'll never forget. I'm so deeply grateful to have had the opportunity to express to my father how much he meant to me, and I am especially grateful to the Power of Clearing process that allowed us both to heal in such a profound way.

Two weeks later, my father went back to the hospital. They couldn't find anything wrong with the valve in his heart. The doctors said it was impossible and that all the previous results must have been incorrect. My father attributed the healing to some vitamin supplements he was taking at the time, but I knew something more tremendously powerful happened on that day at the workshop.

I didn't feel the need to change his view. All I knew was that my father was out of pain and no longer at Death's door. He still had the heart arrhythmia, but his breathing had returned to normal, and, of course, he was delighted to be able to train in his beloved gym again.

The Power of Clearing process was so profound for me that I went on to become a Power of Clearing coach. The valve problem in my father's heart never returned.

Our hearts thrive on love. In the case of the heart, it's been proven by authors such as David Hamilton that loving thoughts, kindness and extending love to others nourishes this vital organ.

My father was a very loving and caring man in so many ways. He was always willing to do someone a favour, especially saving them money by transporting their things in his large van when they needed something delivered or picked up for free. He'd often pick me up if ever I needed him to, and he was always there for his grandsons. He gave an enormous amount of time to the young lads in the gym and showed his love in many other ways. But like many tough men, he found it extremely difficult to express his feelings. While he softened from our healing experience, he also slowly drifted back to his old self, once again putting up a hard, tough exterior. He'd experienced healing but was unable to maintain the change.

About five years after our experience, my father started feeling unwell again. This time, it wasn't the valve, but his heart simply failing and weakening. Love and honesty *can* heal the body, but we must maintain that change in consciousness if we are to *remain* healed.

I'd found two amazing books entitled *How Your Mind Can Heal Your Body* and *Why Kindness Is Good for You* by David Hamilton. His books give scientific evidence that the heart directly responds to loving thoughts, words and actions. I took the books to my father and excitedly shared what I'd discovered.

Instead of being happy, my father reacted very angrily for the first time since our healing. I was shocked and deeply hurt. I went to the door to leave because I was so upset. As I went to shut the door behind me, I heard a voice in my head (which I now know is the voice of Love, beyond ego and fear) say, *Don't just run away. Tell him you only came to share this with him because you love him.* This was the *last* thing I wanted to say while he was shouting at me, but I ignored the fear and spoke the words I was given.

I've never seen anyone shift from rage to calm as quickly as I did that day with my father. He immediately looked down and said, 'I know, but you see...' He paused and said, 'I just can't do what you're suggesting, not in this lifetime.' I suddenly understood why he'd reacted so badly: While he realised what I shared with him from the book was true, he wasn't able to make the change required.

Instead of trying to talk him into it, I respected his honesty and decided in that moment that I had to stop trying to help him around this issue, and instead, I lovingly accepted his decision. I knew the loving response was to allow him that choice, and I knew how hard it would be for him to drop his persona and change. I certainly know how difficult it's been on my own journey to change patterns that I've seen in myself that don't serve me. Expecting someone else to change just because I wanted them to was selfish and would never work.

So many of us fall into the habit of trying to change others instead of putting the focus on ourselves. I'm learning that the greatest influence we can have on others is simply being the example of the change we wish to see in them. Focusing on others and needing them to change is controlling ... and also a way for us to avoid looking at ourselves.

Once I fully accepted what my father said to me and appreciated how honest he'd been with me, we had a really lovely talk. I left feeling calm, peaceful and with a sense of relief. I finally stopped believing it was my responsibility to help him. It was time for me to let go and focus on my own healing journey.

As I left, he repeated some very similar words that he'd spoken when we did the Power of Clearing process:

'I know what you are doing is right, and I admire you.'

I thanked him. I'll never forget those words he shared as I continue this journey to return to Love and as I witness more and more that:

Love Is Truth and Love WILL Set You Free!

After my father left his body, I wrote this poem. It helped me to see death in a more positive light. Once again, I felt it came from a powerful loving consciousness that is far more aware than my logical mind. When a message brings me more peace and acceptance, I trust it is truth.

Death of a Loved One

It's time to see death, through the eyes of all
knowing,
to rejoice and send Love, to the one who is going.

To return to a place, where no one is judged,
to finally realise, we have always been Loved.

Why do we choose, to think death is so wrong,
to be saddened and angry and fear the beyond.

Why do we choose, to feel sadness at death,
and cry at the memories and grasp onto what's
left.

When all they are doing, is packing their bags,
for a far greater place, to a beautiful land.

Where Love is the life force, and joy is what's
breathed,
this we can choose, for our newfound belief.

Why choose the worse one, it's just a sad thought,
one fills us with Love and the other with fraught.

So, you see the experience, is just how you view it,
a thought when it's changed, can simply renew it.

We all have to go, from this world to the next,
So, let's change our minds and have no regrets.

When someone is leaving, send them Love and just
      know,
that their time here is over, they are ready to go.

Don't think as you Love them, you have to
      feel bad,
they don't want to leave you, feeling so sad.

So, love them, be present and allow them to be,
for it's time for their passing, you're setting them
      free.

It's their time to move on now, where one day
      you'll be,
rejoined with your Loved one, for eternity.

Chapter 3

The Miracle of Forgiveness: Healing from Rape

Have you ever caught yourself saying, 'Well, that's unforgivable' or heard someone else say 'I'll never forgive them'? I had an experience that I thought was impossible to forgive, but I was proven wrong.

I won't divulge who the person was, but I will say it was an ex-partner, someone who was supposed to love me ... which, for me, made it so much worse.

I've left out some details because it would reveal who the person was. The most important aspect of this account is to illustrate the power of forgiveness and the miracle of how it occurred.

~

One day, I discovered how much my partner was lying to me when I found out he'd been seeing someone else behind my back. I was extremely hurt and angry when he came to see me that day, so I confronted him with what I knew. I told him the relationship was over and that I would never have sex with him again! He replied, 'I can have sex with you whenever I want.' Before I knew it, I was thrown violently to the floor. He pulled off my clothes from my waist down; it shocked me how quickly and easily he was able to remove them.

I remember I couldn't move any part of my body. He somehow managed to cross my arms over my chest with one hand while his legs were holding down the lower part of my body. This allowed him to have one hand free to remove my clothes. I felt so helpless! I tried to bite the hand that was holding my two arms down, but no matter how hard I tried, I just couldn't reach it. I couldn't believe this person I'd loved so much could be doing this to me.

As soon as it was over, I grabbed my clothes and ran out of the house to a neighbour, where I called the police. My partner was arrested, and, to my surprise, he admitted to the rape. Apparently, he was distressed and regretted the act he'd just committed. A week later, after he'd spoken with a lawyer, he changed his statement and told the police that in our relationship, I liked it when he forced himself on me! Of course, this wasn't true, and it felt like another blow to my heart that he could say such a terrible thing. I was informed of his changed statement by two police officers that came to my door. They also told me I'd have to defend myself in court against this false allegation, and that it would just be my word against his: I would be the one on trial.

I felt hopeless because I knew how convincing he could be and what a great liar he was. I wasn't confident in myself at the time. I didn't feel strong enough to place myself in that position, so I dropped the charge.

Our relationship had been dysfunctional right from the start, but it took the rape for me to realise that, finally, the relationship was over. Unfortunately, even after we split up, there were times I still encountered him because he was involved in some areas of my life. Instead of being kinder to me, he was even more abusive, spreading lies about me to others and generally making my life difficult. All of this fuelled my hatred for him, which continued to consume me for the next eight years.

One day, someone gave me a book entitled *The Little Soul and The Sun* by Neil Donald Walsch. It's a story written for children, about the power of forgiveness, but clearly the messages are for whoever is reading it. The story is of a soul choosing to come to earth to experience forgiveness. It explains how forgiveness is one of our soul's natural qualities. I've come to understand that, as a soul, it's actually natural *not* to judge; in fact, as a soul, we don't even know *how* to judge because we see everything from a higher perspective. So, we choose to come to earth to fully experience forgiving someone to deepen our understanding of what it truly feels like *to* forgive.

It seems particularly hard to forgive some things in the human experience, as we're run by our ego-thinking mind, and we forget how to see things from that higher perspective.

It also becomes very clear that by coming to earth and truly forgiving someone, the soul evolves greatly!

The book begins with a little soul having a conversation with God. The soul expresses that out of all the wonderful qualities of love it knows it is, it wants to experience what it's like to actually *be* forgiveness. God then explains that to truly know yourself as forgiveness, you're going to need another soul to agree to do something terrible to you, so that you have an opportunity to become the experience of forgiveness.

The soul stands in front of an infinite number of other souls, all shining brightly in their glory, radiating the love and light they are. One soul steps forward and says, 'I'll perform this terrible act for you in your next lifetime, but in order to do this, I'll have to dim my light and lower my vibration. Only then will I be able to be the "bad one" who hurts you so deeply.' The little soul is somewhat confused and asks the other soul why they'd be prepared to do this. The other soul replies, 'Because I love you!'

When I read this, I began to tremble, crying from the depths of my soul as the magnitude of what I was reading began to shake me to my core. As more and more tears flowed down my cheeks, I stopped reading, allowing the understanding to become fully realised in my whole being. A definite shift of perspective was occurring inside me as my view of my ex changed in an instant.

In the story, the soul who agreed to perform this malicious act gets a little more serious. It says, 'If I agree to do this terrible deed, I ask of you only one thing: Please don't forget how much I love you! For in the moment that I smite you, I will have forgotten who I truly am, and if you forget too, then we both will be lost.'

When I read these words with my ex-partner in my mind, I realised I'd definitely forgotten the truth of who he was and that, now, we were both indeed completely lost. I cried deeply as compassion returned for him and for what he'd agreed to do for me as a soul. My story of victimhood simply fell away as this profound truth cracked my heart wide open.

The long hatred had been hardening my whole being, and now love had returned. I felt a delicious freedom and peace; no longer was there even an ounce of anger or resentment present. Instead of hatred, I felt an immense sense of gratitude fill my heart for his soul. It was a miracle! To this day, compassion and love remain in my heart for this being. Not a trace of resentment has ever returned.

I immediately knew this didn't mean that I needed or wanted to get close to him again, for he was still deeply troubled. I just knew the hatred I had for him had left me, and I was now finally at peace! I'd experienced a deeper, higher understanding of why the rape occurred, which resulted in this miraculous transformation. What I had also done in that moment was remember who his soul was and the agreement we must have made before coming to earth.

～

Before my shift in consciousness happened, I still had contact with my ex, but after this miraculous forgiveness occurred, instantaneously, he left my life completely. This felt like a second miracle, showing me when we truly forgive something or someone, *everything* shifts arounds us. The problem no longer remains an issue and can leave our lives, as it did for me.-When forgiveness is reached, all our sorrow and pain dissolves, and we set ourselves free!

If you're holding on to any resentment, grievance or hatred for someone, I urge you to read the amazing story *The Little Soul and The Sun* (especially if my experience isn't enough for you to realise that *anything* can be forgiven)! Forgiveness is important because the pain and hatred we feel for someone *will* eventually destroy us and can often even result in physical illness or disease.

Many people hold on to grievance because they believe that if they forgive the person, it means they're condoning the behaviour. But my experience in no way makes rape okay just because an agreement was made before this lifetime! Anything anyone does to deliberately harm another or seek revenge has its own consequences for that being (which could include needing to go to prison).

Forgiveness is an extremely powerful form of Love – ultimately for the one who needs to forgive. No longer is this just a concept for me; I now absolutely know that forgiveness holds the essence of the deepest Love and that:

Love is Truth and Only LOVE Will Set You Free!

I highly recommend reading *The Little Soul and The Sun* by Neil Donald Walsch, as I've paraphrased the message from what I understood of the story. The wording in the actual book is beautiful, powerful and a must-read if you have someone in your life you have not yet forgiven.

Chapter 4

Healing From Bulimia

Part of my healing journey in this lifetime has been specifically about not only healing my own addictions, but also dealing with struggles of addiction in some people around me. There are many forms of addiction, not just to alcohol or drugs. My primary one was worrying about what others thought of me (a huge aspect of co-dependency), which led to years of an addictive eating disorder called bulimia.

Apparently, one of the hardest addictions to break is any form of an eating disorder, because we must learn how to have a new, healthy relationship with food, rather than just cutting it out of our lives completely, as we might with alcohol. If you've ever suffered from an eating disorder and have been told you'll 'never be over it', (as I was told by a so-called 'expert'), I'm living proof that it *is* possible.

For me, bulimia started with needing to look perfect in the eyes of the world. It wasn't just the way I looked that was important but also keeping my weight low, which enabled me to achieve more in my sport. For most of my life, I believed if I wasn't achieving highly at something (or looking good), I wouldn't be loved by my parents *or* the world. Somehow, I concluded that if I was completely unnoticed, I'd end up very lonely. This completely terrified me. The fear drove me to become obsessed with my weight.

When I was almost 14 years old, I took up weight training because my father had a gym. I'd just left springboard diving, a sport I'd competed in for seven years. Although I'd been a national champion in my age group, I *really* grew to hate diving.

I managed to persuade my parents to allow me to stop, but the condition was to start weight training so that I 'wouldn't get fat' (my father's exact words). I was delighted at the thought of 'only' having to lift weights, because being a springboard diver, for me, was extremely scary at times – especially when the dive went wrong. I didn't believe weight training would be nearly as fearful, so I willingly agreed.

I loved training with weights in my father's gym right from the start. It was very social, and I was the only female training along with the guys (another reason to always look my very best and keep myself slim and attractive). Even though I was only 14, I ended up dating a good-looking guy from the gym.

Within a few short months, I was lifting weight that qualified me to compete in the British championships. I was 15 years old, weighing only 44kg (96 pounds). Despite being the youngest in the competition, I won the gold medal in my class. This qualified me to go to the world championship in Hawaii. It was an amateur sport; if I could raise the money (or get a sponsor), then I could go with the team. This was the chance of a lifetime!

My parents had only ever been able to afford to take us on one-week camping holidays each year (or on a canal boat before it became too expensive). While I loved those holidays, this championship in Hawaii was an opportunity that I'd never dreamed of. After a lot of consideration, my father decided it was worth applying for a bank loan, and he decided to make it a family holiday. He was loaned two thousand pounds, which enabled my mother and sister to join us. It was one of the best family holidays I ever had: We got to stay in Hawaii for a week after the competition ended. My father was so proud of me because I placed third in the competition for my class. I returned home with a trophy as tall as I was. I was hooked!

I continued to win the British championships year after year, still lifting in a very light bodyweight class. But it was becoming harder and harder to stay at that weight. I was very careful about what I ate, aware I had to stay in the same bodyweight class I'd originally qualified for, or I couldn't compete in next year's world championships.

My monthly periods stopped by the time I was 15. I'd often get light-headed. I had almost no fat on my body; looking back, this was probably why my periods stopped.

At 17 years old, I was lifting in another world championship in Australia. Having practically starved myself up until then, I allowed myself to eat whatever I wanted at the banquet afterward. Because my stomach had shrunk from restricting my food intake for so long, I found myself in excruciating pain. My roommate suggested (quite nonchalantly) putting my fingers down my throat to make myself vomit. She said she did it all the time – that was how she kept her weight down. I thought it was ridiculous, but the pain got so bad, I decided to try it.

Immediately, I felt relief. It was so easy to do! I distinctly remember thinking, 'Well, that's handy. If I ever eat too much, I can just make myself sick'. It only took another three months for it to become a habit I couldn't stop.

I found myself constantly overeating and making myself vomit. It became a vicious cycle: Making myself sick created an even greater hunger that caused me to overeat again at the next meal. I'd feel almost starving within an hour or two, after bringing up all that I'd just eaten from the previous meal.

Then, I became addicted to laxatives. Vomiting wasn't enough to relieve the fear of gaining weight. I began to take more and more of them, way over the amount prescribed on the bottle. I was training hard and maintaining the same body weight, but no one knew the struggle I was going through. I felt extremely ashamed (back then, eating disorders weren't considered an illness, but were looked at as a shameful, selfish act), and I knew my father would *not* understand.

Life started to become unbearable. I couldn't enjoy eating food anymore and I was constantly feeling ashamed. Not telling anyone I had an eating disorder meant I was carrying that burden all by myself. I was depressed and often felt like giving up on life. Every morning, I'd pray, *God, please help me to not overeat today.* Every day, I'd fail. I desperately longed to just be able to eat like everyone else!

One day, I overdosed on laxatives and found myself in tremendous pain, sweat pouring from me as I sat on the toilet. I eventually collapsed on the floor in the bathroom and cried out to God:

Please God, this is not a life I want to live anymore. I just want to die.

Then, I heard a voice within my own mind (which I now know to be the voice of Love) say, *Get rid of the laxatives. They are killing you. Allow yourself to be sick. You are trying to get over this overnight and you are setting yourself up for failure.* The voice was kind and gentle, loving and compassionate. It wasn't a voice I'd heard before. The voice in my mind that I was familiar with was always telling me how bad and useless I was, asking why couldn't I just stop doing this and be like everyone else?

In this state of utter desperation (or, surrender), I listened to the advice I was hearing from this new voice. I threw the laxatives in the trash, never touching them again. As I walked over to the sink, the voice continued. *See if you can refrain from making yourself sick just once a week to start with. When you do manage to do this – even just once – you will know it's possible and that you can do it again. Focus only on the positive and give yourself a pat on the back when you don't make yourself sick. Don't focus on the times that you do.*

I realised the voice was giving me *very* small steps to follow, because by this time I'd been making myself sick about eight times a day. This new voice was patient, kind and it knew me. It knew exactly how to communicate with me – by using the very words I'd understand.

I didn't realise at the time how long it would take to completely stop overeating and making myself vomit. It was slow and gradual as the times between making myself sick became longer and longer.

One day, when I was about to make myself throw up, the voice spoke again: *Don't throw all of it up. You can keep some in without gaining weight.* Another time, it said, *Don't make* any *food wrong.* At the time, I had a mental list of all the foods I shouldn't eat. It was all part of my food obsession. If I broke one of my rules by eating something that I was desperately trying not to eat, I'd say to myself, *You've failed again, so you may as well eat more and more of it* . And then, of course, I'd vomit again. But when I stopped making some foods good and some foods bad, I stopped overeating. If I really wanted something, I'd allow myself to have it without condemnation or feeling guilty; subsequently, there was no need to punish myself by eating too much of it.

To put it another way, I found that without creating rules about food, I no longer had rules to break.

It took five years to completely heal from my eating disorder. One day, I realised I'd broken the habit completely: The compulsion to overeat and then vomit was gone. That loving voice, which spoke to me when I truly surrendered, was powerful and deeply compassionate, able to override my ego's voice of condemnation and shame. Many refer to this loving voice as the Holy Spirit.

I've come to realise, after speaking with hundreds of people who have recovered from addictions, that our real problem is our 'stinking thinking' that we *identify* with over time. When drugs and alcohol are involved, they exacerbate ego-thinking and self-loathing. All addiction is simply an effect of the *real* problem – a lack of self-love, caused by listening to the wrong voice.

Most of us have to fully surrender before we can allow Love in enough for us to change. Once I hit rock bottom and cried out for help, I became open to Divine intervention. For me, that Divine intervention manifested as an inner voice. For everyone, though, once you get to a point of total helplessness, Divine intervention *will* show up in a way that's perfect for you. It's in our helplessness – which is really surrender – that we become willing to ask for help and actually receive it. That point at which we finally surrender to something greater than ourselves can't be forced on anyone. It must be desired.

The miracle for me was not just that I was helped when I finally surrendered and called out to God, but that, to this day, I still have a healthy relationship with food. I allow myself to eat whatever I want; over the last 28 years, I've naturally begun to eat healthier and healthier. I don't have a desire to eat meat in my daily diet, but I *would* if I really wanted to. I don't call myself a vegetarian, vegan or any other label. I make no rules for myself around food. Life is good, and I'm truly grateful for that loving voice I now call my higher Self, God, Love or Truth.

If you're struggling with an addiction, please don't despair. You *will* recover when the time is right and in a way that's totally unique to you. One thing I am one hundred percent sure of is that God loves each and every one of us, whether we're in addiction or not. We're *so* deeply loved regardless of whether or not we're achieving anything ... and God *definitely* loves us regardless of what we look like!

Universal Love is just *waiting* for us to ask for help from a place of total surrender and trust in it. For me, God's will *is* that Universal Love ... but it's a Love that's *way* beyond what our small ego can comprehend.

We are *all* meant to have a connection to that source of Love. Without it, we struggle more in life than we need to. But when we become more connected to our eternal, divine, Loving source, we become more loving toward ourselves and others.

Love is the most powerful healer. That is why the essence of a miracle is *always* loving and why:

Love Is Truth and LOVE Will Set You Free!

Chapter 5

Healing Money Fears

Not one person I've spoken to over the years, all across the globe, has been without some kind of fear surrounding money. Maybe you're someone who has difficulty spending money, so you find yourself hoarding it or 'saving it for a rainy day'. Even those with lots of money say they fear losing what they have, or fear what they *do* have is never enough.

I'm not suggesting there aren't some beings on this planet who haven't overcome their issues with money, but in general, it's a common fear: We believe that without money, we'll be homeless ... or even die. It's a fear that often drives us unconsciously, affecting our daily choices.

Have you had similar fears, even when you had a good-paying job and plenty of money in the bank? I *definitely* have!

∾

I often made choices about money from fear, as my mind would bring up 'what if' questions around not having enough in the future. These thoughts would plague me, and, of course, they were a thousand times stronger if anything was already not going well financially.

I wasn't constantly having thoughts about losing everything and being homeless on the street, but I came to realise so many of my little fears were driven by this underlying belief that if I spent *any* amount of money, I wouldn't have enough later on. I overreacted to situations involving money which manifested in lots of different ways: If I purchased something for myself that wasn't a necessity, I'd feel guilty. If the guilt was strong, I'd return it the next day for a refund. My family used to tease me about this pattern, as it happened so often.

I found it difficult to enjoy the money I *did* have. I very rarely treated myself. I didn't like depending on others for money – not even my husband. I was a housewife and mother and wanted to be available to pick my children up from school and be with them during their term holidays. The only jobs that made this possible were low-paid and part-time. I loved being a mother, but not being able to earn much money added to my fear about spending it freely.

I wasn't a 'career woman'; the message from my parents was that I'd find a husband to take care of me – my role was to be a good wife and mother. My father, who was my weightlifting coach, wanted to support me financially so that I could dedicate myself to the sport. So, after finishing school, I only needed a part-time job. I worked in a pub, which was great fun, but not something that paid well. This lack of career experience added to my belief that I couldn't support myself financially.

Years later, after being married and divorced and recognising that I was much more than my beliefs, I noticed how I could become totally overwhelmed by fear in certain financial circumstances. If I was charged more than I was expecting to pay for anything, I'd be overwhelmed by fear. One day, while feeling intensely anxious, I dropped to my knees and, with all my heart, prayed to be freed from all fear around financial 'lack'.

Several years later, I wanted to travel the world. I decided to sell my house without purchasing another one. This wasn't an easy decision; I had a *very* comfortable life. I had no mortgage and plenty of money coming in from the rooms I rented out in my home. But something inside me just knew there was more to life than this.

My children didn't live with me anymore, so I was free to pursue my dreams. Still, it took me five more years to muster up the courage to make this change. I was conflicted about putting my house up for sale. When I finally accepted an offer, I'd wake up every morning feeling terrified, my mind consumed with doubt. After weeks of this torment, I withdrew the house from the market ... but instead of feeling relieved, I felt a deep, sinking feeling in my heart and soul. It became unbearable and felt even worse than the initial fearful thoughts of selling my home. Eventually, even though

I was still feeling fearful, I followed my heart and went ahead with the house sale.

My plan was to travel around the world and see what life might have in store for me besides wandering around a large house feeling there must be more to life. I knew that change creates change, so the bigger the change I made, the more my life and beliefs would have to shift. I trusted that by leaving my old way of life behind, it would open up more opportunities for growth, expansion and healing.

With the house sold, I had a lot of money in the bank. A friend suggested investing it with the help of a financial adviser. I wasn't a gambler, so I chose the lowest-risk investment option, keeping some money back for living expenses as I travelled. A few months later, I found myself staying with a spiritual teacher and his wife in the United States. I was having the time of my life being with people I felt understood me and who encouraged me to love myself and truly have fun.

One morning, completely out of the blue, I awoke feeling the most intense fear. I had a thought: What if I lost all the money I'd just invested? A terrified feeling shuddered through my body. I felt physically sick. In that moment, I truly believed without that money I would surely die! The feeling of fear was so awful that I immediately told myself I needed to go back to the UK and take all the money out of the investment and distribute it into several banks. I told the friends I was staying with what was going on for me and how dreadful I felt. I acknowledged that I didn't want to leave and go back to the UK, but I needed to get rid of this terrible feeling.

I realised this had been a pattern of mine – needing to get rid of fear *immediately*, even if it meant doing something I didn't really want to do. Explaining this, my friend suggested I do something different this time. He asked me to breathe *with* the fear and feel it fully instead of running away from it.

My ego shouted at me, 'No, don't do this, just leave now and secure the money.' But something deep inside me knew I had to face this fear and not run. So, I did as he suggested and stayed with the fear when it arose. The intense fear kept coming in waves when I thought about losing it all. Over and over again, it would arise. Each time, I'd start to breathe deeply and feel the fear fully. I'd invite the fear in and say, 'I really want to feel you. Give me more.' I started to welcome it rather than push it away.

As I breathed with the fear, it would intensify, but I just kept breathing it in more and more deeply. Each wave of fear would reach a peak and then start to subside until it disappeared completely. This continued for another two days. It would've been easy to give up, but I was determined to see it through. Something deep down told me it wouldn't last.

Halfway through the third day, I noticed I wasn't feeling the fear anymore. I deliberately thought about the money I had invested, and nothing happened. No fear arose at all. I couldn't believe it! I couldn't contact those fearful feelings even when I tried. And it only took three days! This was a complete miracle; it was the first time I didn't change anything outside myself to try and get rid of fear. Instead, I welcomed it, and embraced it, full on.

This didn't make sense to my logical mind, but the

process really worked! I realised the fear I was feeling felt like a bullying kind of energy. The more I feared it, the more it persisted and got a hold on me. I've seen that bullies only bully those who fear them; that's the only way they're able to continue feeling powerful and in control. It's the same with our own fear. What a revelation.

I never went back to the UK to take out the money I'd invested, which allowed me to pursue my dreams and follow my heart.

How many times do we fail to follow our true desires because of fear? After all, most of us only allow ourselves to feel a little bit of pain before we try to shut it down again. But any emotion that feels uncomfortable – like sadness, anger, shame, doubt or guilt – just needs to be welcomed and felt fully until it subsides. Deep breathing helps us embrace these feelings more deeply and quickly. It's best to cry as hard and long as you need when sadness arises, in order to feel it fully.

I find it helpful to go somewhere where no one can hear me and cry and scream as loud as I need to until I'm exhausted and have nothing left in me. It's amazingly cathartic but not something most of us were allowed or encouraged to do as children. Instead, we carry buried emotions inside us which fester like open wounds of pain. This can lead to many different types of addictions: We find different ways to distract ourselves from feeling pain by using things like alcohol, drugs, food, sex, shopping or busyness (like watching TV or going on the computer, playing video games or becoming a workaholic – anything rather than feel things deeply).

This is also why depression is such a rapidly growing problem. In my experience, depression is mainly caused by suppression of expression: After repeatedly stuffing emotions down, we come to a breaking point where they can't be suppressed any longer. Crying is one way our body starts to heal, by letting out some of these suppressed feelings. Depression often *forces* us to cry. I know; I've experienced it.

I was depressed in my mid-thirties; I'd become a master at controlling my emotions. I believed that expressing sadness or getting angry was either wrong or a weakness. I spent years suppressing my anger, fears and sadness to fit in and be liked. I even discovered that being too *joyful* can make some people uncomfortable, so I trained myself to tone down my joy.

But through this process of really meeting fear head-on and feeling it fully, I finally realised that running from my emotions was not the answer. Today, I'll sometimes still react, but am getting better at just feeling the fear and moving *through* it, rather than pushing it away. I accept my human journey; I know it's about progress, not perfection.

Life gives us choices. We have free will to *choose* how we feel and act; it's a God-given quality we *all* possess. When our choices don't bring us peace, we can either judge ourselves (or others), *or* we can learn from the choices we've made. Judging *anything* as 'wrong' is *not* Love in action.

Once we feel a painful emotion arising, it's vital that we *fully* feel it, or we can't truly let it go. Stuffing emotions down once they're present isn't healthy. This doesn't mean we get to project our emotions onto others or tell ourselves they're bad or wrong! In fact, when we *allow* ourselves to fully feel our negative feelings, it *stops* us projecting them onto others.

Love embraces all things knowing there's value in every experience. When we look through the eyes of Love, we *always* find gratitude, because:

Love Is Truth and Truth WILL Set You Free!

Chapter 6

A Homeless Angel

I've talked about how hard it was to let go of the house I loved so much to explore a new way of living and being in the world. My greatest fear surrounding not having a home was of ending up with nothing and living on the street.

But after selling my house, I walked out my front door for the very last time and didn't look back. I walked towards my very small, but fully loaded, car and said goodbye to where I'd lived for 13 years. I felt surprisingly joyful and excited about diving into the unknown (despite waking up every morning for the past three months racked with fear). I had some plans of my own (travelling to Bali), but I was also open to whatever opportunities might come my way. I now had no ties to any one place. From that moment, I started living one day at a time.

∾

My first plan was to drive to Teignmouth in Devon and stay with a lovely friend for a few weeks before heading to the US to visit a friend in North Carolina, followed by a healing workshop in Maui.

I arrived in Teignmouth that first evening, totally exhausted. My friend had put out a mattress for me on the floor of their attic. I'd gone from living in a beautiful, fully paid-for, four-bedroom home to sleeping on a mattress on the floor ... and all I felt was a surreal sense of freedom. I was more excited than scared, which surprised me: I'd spent the last year going in and out of intense fear over this decision, but once it became my reality, I was calm and simply looking forward to the unknown.

I awoke the following day feeling immense joy, more joyful than ever before. I couldn't understand it. It just wasn't what I had envisaged.

I decided to make the ten-minute walk to the nearby beach. The sun was shining brightly; it was a wonderful morning. I had a huge smile on my face and a skip in my step as I approached the beach.

I saw a man sitting on a low wall playing a ukulele while singing a line from the Beatles –'love, love me do'. He stopped singing as I walked past, and he said with a big smile, 'What a beautiful day it is!' I agreed and smiled back as I started to go down the steps that led to the beach. I then noticed he had a small sleeping roll next to him and a hat out for receiving money. He was so friendly and happy, I hoped he'd still be there when I came back so I could give him some money.

As I walked along the beach, I remembered I'd wanted to

get over my fear of talking to homeless people on the street. For some reason that I didn't understand at the time, I found myself almost embarrassed to stop and make conversation with homeless people. It wasn't that I was afraid they would hurt me, but not knowing what to say to them. I also realised I was worried about what people would think about me if I was to sit down next to someone who was homeless and have a conversation. As I walked back towards where the man was sitting, I was determined to get over this uneasiness. The only way was to just do it.

The man was still there, singing the same song about love, so I sat right next to him on the wall and asked him how long he'd been homeless as I, too, was now without a home of my own. He told me he'd been living on the streets for about eight years. His relationship had crumbled, and his job had been very unfulfilling. He'd become disillusioned with the 'rat race' of working just to pay bills. When his relationship ended, he decided to sell his house, walking away with 15 thousand pounds. He said it lasted him about a year, and then he became homeless by choice, as he didn't want to return to his old way of living.

He told me he was very happy sleeping under the stars at night and said God was taking care of him because in his eight years of living on the street, he'd never gone hungry. He said he'd only ever had to eat out of a bin once, and the food was something thrown out from a shop because it was out of date. He just kept saying how grateful he was to be alive, and that Love is the answer to everything. He asked me my name, then said, 'Rosie-Maria, the world is going to change, and Love is the answer.'

His name was Haggis.

We talked for about 15 minutes. The more he spoke, the more my body filled with an unbelievable joy. He told me he didn't drink or take drugs, and every opportunity he had he would try to help others on the street know they didn't need to drink, either. He explained that some people he could help, but some weren't ready to hear there was another way.

Haggis' nature was so beautiful. It was as if he was showing me that, with love and gratitude in your heart, nothing else matters; even living on the street can be a wonderful, joyful life. To this day, I can honestly say that he is the happiest, most grateful, love-filled man I've ever had the privilege to meet. He kept saying, 'peace and love to the world'. He told me I was on a journey, and I would find what I was looking for. He said we were meant to meet that day to have this talk together. He went on to say, 'I hope that your path is rich with love and happiness', to which I replied, 'Well, your life certainly seems to be that way.'

Haggis continued to explain that no one (and no thing) could take anything from him because he has love in his heart. He said the world is going to change soon because we can't go on treating each other the way we have been. 'Remember my words, Rosie-Maria. We need to love and help each other.' Then he laughed and said we need to put a smile on our face and spread happiness. The whole time Haggis spoke, he had a smile on his face. He lit me up with his words and his amazing joyful energy; I felt transformed in his presence.

What was the chance of meeting a man like that the very day after walking away from my house *and* carrying a huge inner fear of being homeless? I truly believe he was sent to me to show me that even my worst fear was not necessary or how I'd imagined it to be ... especially *this* homeless man, who had love and appreciation for the whole world in his heart. I've met some very rich people in my life that were nowhere near as happy as Haggis was (and nowhere near as grateful and loving).

I thanked Haggis for sharing his journey with me and gave him a big hug. I took a ten-pound note out of my purse and handed it to him, telling him to have a great meal on me. He didn't want to accept it, saying that me talking to him had made his day. I insisted he take it and told him he had *definitely* made mine!

As I walked away, Haggis shouted out to me in a loving, gentle voice, 'I love you, Rosie-Maria.' I smiled and said thank you as my eyes welled up with tears of joy. I felt I'd been in the presence of an angel; my whole body was lit up with love.

I went back the next day to see if I could speak with Haggis again, as I had many more questions for him. He wasn't there, so I drove around Teignmouth for a while, asking locals if they'd seen a homeless man playing a ukulele. No one had seen anyone matching that description. To this day, I wonder if he *was* sent to me – an angel in disguise.

∽

Although I still had a lot to heal around my own fear of being without money, Haggis showed me that his trust in his God and love for love itself contained more freedom and security than any amount of money could bring.

Haggis was a demonstration that Love is Truth, and it definitely set him free!

Chapter 7

Living One Year Without My Own Money

Have you ever felt *proud* of yourself for never having to ask anyone for money? Have you ever thought you'd rather die than have to ask *anyone* for *any* help, *especially* for money?

Many of us carry a great fear of rejection; we'd rather keep doing something we don't like or that's become difficult just in case we're rejected if we *do* ask for help. For many of us, this fear of asking for help unconsciously drives many of our decisions. And it's not just asking for financial help we fear – we struggle in general to share any of our troubles: We'll stay in unhealthy relationships or jobs we hate rather than reaching out for assistance. So many of us have such a resistance towards asking for help that we end up continuously struggling until maybe we find ourselves getting very ill. Then, we *have* to accept help from others because we can't take care of ourselves.

It makes life much less painful if we can learn to ask for help *before* becoming unwell. It's a common belief that to feel worthy, we must do everything by ourselves, causing us to isolate instead of reaching out. If only we could be more vulnerable with each other and give our friends the opportunity to give us their support when we need it. I'm not saying everyone who doesn't ask for help *will* get ill, but it *is* something I've witnessed for many people on this life's journey ... and for myself.

About two months after I'd first healed my fear about not having enough money, more financial fears started to surface. It was fortunate that when these fears arose, I was staying with a friend who'd helped me before. He suggested I sit and breathe with my fear and ask what would help me heal *all* my fears around money. He reminded me to ask the Divine Love within me (God) for the answer. He wasn't religious (and neither was I), but we both believe in Jesus and in his true message to humanity – to love one another and overcome fear with love. I was familiar with asking God for help, as I believe in a Creator, or Source of unconditional love that abides within us all.

When my friend invited me to ask God for an answer, I was afraid at first. What if God told me to give all my money away? I expressed this concern to my friend, and he replied, 'Don't worry. You don't have to do what God suggests if you aren't ready for it.' So, I started to breathe and ask God what it would take to be free from *all* my fears around money. At first, I didn't receive an answer. Feeling about ready to give up, my friend patiently encouraged me to keep on breathing and trusting. Suddenly, what came to mind was an answer that felt just as terrifying as the answer I'd feared. It felt so utterly ridiculous that I refused to speak the message out loud.

But the message I so clearly received was:

Live an entire year without touching any of the money you have from the sale of your house.

Basically, start living as if I had nothing. Immediately, I felt overwhelming fear. I started to share the message I'd received with my friend, but as soon as I began, I burst into tears. I shouted, 'I can't possibly do this! I'd have to ask people to feed me and house me when I have all this money in the bank. That's just ridiculous!' I thought that everyone I asked would hate me and be resentful towards me for asking such a thing. I thought I'd lose all my friends, and no one would want to help me.

I was afraid this message was coming from my ego to try and stop me from spending the money I had and felt others would also think the same thing, judging me terribly. *They'll just say it's my ego talking, not God.* I couldn't stop crying at the thought of doing what I'd been told. Yet, despite all the fear it brought up in me, something deep down told me the message was *not* from ego.

Over the years, I've discovered that the ego voice talks us

into staying in our comfort zone ... and this message was definitely *not* doing that. In fact, it was the opposite – I'd have to face my fears.

After lots of supportive questions from my friend, I saw that if I did what was being asked of me, I'd have an opportunity to heal far more than just my fear around being without money: I'd have to swallow my pride and trust that I'd be taken care of, even if I didn't use the money I already had. I'd have to fully put my trust in God and find enough self-worth to ask for help.

My friend then said something that touched me deeply: 'Did you know a practice of the Essenes was to go on the streets with a begging bowl and walk in the shoes of one who has nothing'? (He was referring to a community of people called the Essenes who lived during the time of Jesus. It's said that Jesus lived with the Essenes for a while. They were dedicated to God and to becoming totally unselfish). This practice of begging in the streets was a way to learn humility.

I needed time to assimilate what had been suggested. I thought about it for about a week, feeling whether I had the courage to go through with it. I felt all the fears the mind brought forth (including the possibility I may have to spend some time on the street if I were to commit to living a whole year without touching the money I had). I finally made the decision after contacting another spiritual teacher I fully trusted. I asked them if they felt this message was coming from Love or my ego.

In almost the exact same words my other friend had used, they said this would help me heal far more than just my fears around money. And did I know a practice of the Essenes was to go out on the streets with a begging bowl?

It felt like God was speaking through my friends directly to me. My trusted friend asked if I was willing to give God the chance to love me. I said emphatically, 'But it will be *people* I'll have to ask, not God!' He replied calmly, 'Rosie-Maria, are you willing to let God love you *through* people? What better way can God give to you but through the love of others, without you needing to offer anything in return?'

I began to sob uncontrollably; I knew how hard it would be for me to receive help, *especially* in the form of money from others. But at the same time, I knew that, in order to heal, I had to accept the challenge God had laid before me. God had indeed spoken to me, and I was going to say yes, no matter where the journey would take me.

I thanked my respected teacher and slowly walked up the stairs to my other friend's living room where he was teaching a group of about 20 people. I sat down quietly in the back where it was dark, tears streaming down my face. My whole body shook at the thought of stepping into this journey straight away, but I knew I couldn't put it off one moment longer, or I'd *never* do it.

I was flying the next day from North Carolina to Rhode Island to stay with another dear friend for a month. I'd already paid for the flight, so that wasn't an issue. I thought I'd need about 20 dollars to buy some food at the airport.

When the talk ended, I very hesitantly raised my hand and asked my friend if I could ask everyone there a question. He immediately invited me to the front and gave me his microphone. I'd been hoping I could do the asking as quietly as possible; with the microphone before me, it proved even more terrifying. That was one of the most difficult moments of my life. I was going to ask these people (only some of whom I knew) if they would help me get through the next day by giving me some money. My mouth went completely dry, my heart beating so hard I thought I was going to have a heart attack. It was proving to be far more difficult than I thought.

My whole body shook so hard it was visible to everyone. I was about to give up, but instead I asked them to give me a moment while I took some deep breaths. Eventually, I told them about the guidance I'd received and about how much money I already had in the bank from the sale of my house. I wanted to be completely transparent and honest. As I came to the point where I was going to ask if each person could maybe give me just one dollar to get me through the next day, my lip began to quiver, and I started to shake again. I paused. How I got those words out, I'll never know.

As I finished speaking, my teacher friend, who'd been present with me when I first heard the message, came running over and hugged me, delighted I was actually going to do it! As he wrapped his arms around me, I cried with relief as I felt his love and encouragement. Then, one after another, people came up to hug me and give me money, some crying with me as they shared their delight in being part of my journey. I couldn't believe the response I was receiving. When I opened my hands, I realized I was holding about six hundred dollars! All I had asked for was one dollar from each person, but I'd received so much more.

And that was just the beginning.

The following day, I sat on the plane wondering how I was going to tell my friend in Rhode Island what my new plans were – living a whole year trusting that I would be fully provided for. I felt rich now that I had the six hundred dollars, but I believed I was going to have to be very careful with it to see how long I could make it last. I still didn't want to ask for help and didn't relish the thought of asking for money again. It never occurred to me I might receive more money and help without even having to ask for it.

My friend picked me up from the airport. I waited until we got to her house to tell her what I was going to do for that year and that I'd already been given six hundred dollars. Her face lit up with joy. She was so excited for me, she immediately declared that I wouldn't have to worry about paying for anything while I was staying with her for the month. She even offered me some vouchers for TK Maxx and asked if she could take me shopping for clothes the next day. I couldn't believe it – she wasn't in judgment of me at all!

All these fearful thoughts I had about how people would react were simply *not* coming true. Instead, my beautiful friend was trying to find even more ways to support me! I felt like crying and thanked her wholeheartedly. I told her that letting me stay with her and feeding me was all I could possibly accept and that I was overwhelmed by her love and support. She took my hands, looked into my eyes, and said, 'Please let me do this for you. Please let me treat you with these vouchers.' In that moment, I received a gift I'll never forget: I realised by not accepting her generosity, I'd keep my dear friend from experiencing the joy of extending her Love. *I* was giving *her* a gift, too.

The next day, I clearly heard a quiet, inner voice say to me, *Offer to do a workshop, by donation only.* I'd co-facilitated many workshops before, leading breathwork, laughter yoga and channelling sessions, but had never actually done one by myself. I longed to start giving my own workshops to help people connect to the Love they are, but I hadn't had the courage to do them by myself. I mentioned the idea to my friend; almost before I finished my sentence, she was on the phone contacting people to invite them.

Within 24 hours, there were ten people wanting to attend, but the only time they could all come was that weekend, giving me only four days to prepare. Everything was happening so quickly, but I chose to act upon this inner voice. I was nervous but also excited at this wonderful opportunity. I told myself it didn't matter if I didn't receive much money in donations, because it would be a great opportunity for me to start doing workshops on my own.

I decided to give a two-day workshop and knew exactly what I was going to offer – the opportunity for participants to heal their blocks to love through powerful methods I'd experienced myself. The workshop was a great success and many beautiful healings occurred. Everyone wrote wonderful testimonials, and I was over the moon that I'd had the courage to say 'yes'.

I left a little box out for donations and thanked everyone for trusting me and giving me this wonderful opportunity to share my gifts with them. I chose to not look inside the box until everyone left. I was stunned when I finally opened it. There was two thousand dollars! Once again, I was brought to tears. Within one week of starting the year as if I had no money, I had two thousand, six hundred dollars! It felt like I was in a dream; this was the complete *opposite* to what I'd expected.

Several people who came to the workshop called me afterwards wanting to take me to lunch. Some of them booked one-on-one sessions with me for channellings, and more money just kept flowing in. They seemed to be in awe of my courage and just wanted to keep giving in all kinds of ways to support my journey. That month was one of the greatest experiences of my life.

It wasn't about the money, but about the amount of love I received from so many beautiful souls. It gave me the trust I needed to face the 11 months that followed.

At the end of my month's stay in Rhode Island, I returned to stay with my spiritual teacher friend in North Carolina. He talked about a pilgrimage to Israel he was going on and mentioned it was fully booked. I commented I was glad there were no spaces left, because I would've been very tempted to join him. I thought no more of it as I climbed into bed that night. Little did I know that after this passing comment, my friend immediately contacted the organiser and asked them to let him know if a space became available.

He received a reply right away that someone had just

dropped out. In the morning, my friend informed me of this. He was so excited about me possibly going, but I was horrified. I had around two thousand six hundred dollars, but the pilgrimage cost five thousand. I felt terrified at the thought of spending all I had and going down to zero again. I also had no idea how I'd raise the rest of the money. I made it very clear I wasn't going to ask for money so I could go on a pilgrimage. I had accepted that there would be times I may have to ask for food and shelter because these things were considered a necessity, but I was *not* going to ask for money for what most people would consider just a holiday.

My friend, who'd become my spiritual mentor, asked me if perhaps this was the next challenging step on my journey. He suggested it takes courage to ask for more than just what's considered a 'necessity', and asked if I was ready to receive even more from God through others. I really didn't want to hear this. Again, I had to sit, breathe and deeply feel into whether I could ask for more money.

The woman organising the pilgrimage offered me a two hundred dollar discount, as she, too, wanted to support my journey. She also gave me two months to try to raise the money before she would need to open the space up for someone else. I could see I was already receiving the help that would enable me to go. But by the end of the week, I had a very bad headache and began to feel quite ill as I contemplated having to ask for money for this trip to Israel. My friend helped me discover that I was literally making myself sick with my own thinking: I was feeling so guilty about asking for assistance that I was beating myself up with my thoughts. That's what was actually causing the head pain.

When I saw my negative thoughts were creating my headache, I decided to override what my mind was saying to me and go ahead and ask for help despite the fear I was feeling. Just after I decided to go ahead with it, my mind screamed at me, *You're going to die if you do this and you'll lose all your friends!* In that moment, I realised my mind was telling me a lie. There was *no way* I was going to die just by asking for help, and I knew I wouldn't lose all my friends. The next day, I emailed everyone I knew, asking if they would help me financially so I could go on this pilgrimage.

I made it very clear I *did* have money but that I'd received guidance to live for one year without touching it, helping me overcome my fear that I'd die if I lost it all. I also told them how hard it was for me to ask for money for something other than just food and shelter. I asked if they'd be willing to share with me any judgments that might arise about my request. I wanted the opportunity to breathe with my reaction to each judgement and (hopefully) further my healing process. Deep down, I knew *I* would probably have been triggered if I'd received an email from someone asking for money under the same circumstances. I was willing to face the judgements being projected onto me from others, in order to heal the same judgements I so clearly had within myself.

I remember my hand hovering over the send button as all my fears rushed into my mind again. Despite my pounding heart, I closed my eyes and sent it. With bated breath I waited for a reply. I sent the email to about 70 people, some of whom I hadn't been in touch with for years.

The first reply wished me all the luck but said they didn't

feel able to send me money. But then I started receiving really encouraging emails, some from friends I'd only met once. They were very excited about my journey and pleased to send me some money, as they admired my courage. I also received emails from about five friends who judged my decision as coming from ego. This was hard to hear – it brought up my worst fears. One email was particularly harsh and angry, bringing up great emotional pain within me, but I managed to overcome the pain by taking some deep breaths until I returned to peace. Once I became calm again, I wrote back with great love, thanking them for being honest with me about how they felt.

Over the next couple of months, I received many donations. The largest one was for two hundred dollars; most ranged from 10 to 50 dollars. Most people didn't respond at all. Then I received a miracle. One of the women who sent me a condemning email at the beginning wrote to me again. This time, she thanked me. She said my email made her so angry, she realised she had to look within herself to see why it had elicited so much anger in her. She didn't go into details about her findings, but she did share that she was grateful for what it had triggered in her; she'd discovered an unconscious fear that was causing her to be judgemental, and she'd experienced great healing from this revelation. She said she was *so* grateful that she now wanted to send me some money towards my trip and wished me much love and a great journey. When I read her words, I wept with relief and joy. I couldn't believe the healing that was happening for others, not just for myself!

Two months later, the night before I was to contact the

organiser of the pilgrimage to let them know if I'd raised enough money to go, I was still one thousand five hundred dollars short. I started to feel really sad, my negative mind telling me I should never have sent the email out in the first place; what was I thinking? Clearly, I wasn't meant to go, or I would've raised all the money in time. Then, suddenly, I felt a sense of peace come over me as I had another thought: What if sending the email out was just about getting me to move through my fears? What if I was never meant to actually go on the pilgrimage? What if I could just be happy with myself for having had the courage to ask?

A soft warmth flooded my body and I felt immense joy. Just before I went to sleep, I said, *God, if you want me to go on this pilgrimage, then I need a miracle.* As I closed my eyes, I took pleasure in knowing I'd send all the money back to my friends who had donated towards the trip. I also took some comfort in knowing I wouldn't have to use up all the money I'd raised with my workshop.

The next morning, I awoke joyfully and went to notify the organisers of the pilgrimage that I wouldn't be going. Just before doing so, I opened some emails that had come in during the night. To my utter amazement, someone I'd met only once sent me one thousand dollars for the trip, and two other people I hardly knew also sent me one hundred and 25 euros each. I trembled with excitement, in sheer awe that God really does exist and works miracles. He'd directly answered my prayer. Even more amazing, when I contacted the woman who sent me the thousand dollars, she told me she'd heard a loud voice telling her she had to give me exactly that amount. She explained that she'd *never* given this amount of money to anyone before, but a feeling of urgency came over her, and she couldn't say no to the request. I later figured out this happened at almost the same time I'd called out to God for a miracle.

This miracle I'll never forget. It changed my life forever; the pilgrimage brought many people into my life that I'm still friends with today. It's also a constant reminder for me that God is real, and the stronger my trust is in God, the more God can help me. Our trust in God is like a bridge to the Divine. It enables a loving power (God) to help us. If we follow what's received, it'll always be for our greater good. For God is Love.

When it looked like I wasn't going to be able to go on the pilgrimage, and my ego first spoke telling me I'd failed, it caused great pain. When I looked at the situation differently and brought love and total acceptance to what was unfolding, God was able to work a miracle. This was the greatest gift I received that whole year of living as if I had no money. I got to experience how the less I tried to control my life and surrendered to what was, the greater the gifts unfolded.

This has been my lived experience: When I truly surrender to *God's* plan ... when my plan doesn't work ... God then has the chance to work amazing miracles. When I put my trust in God in difficult times, I benefit immediately. Peace returns because I let go of struggling, and I find very quickly that things start 'working out' again. For me, God isn't a man in the sky but a presence of Love that's within me, around me and available to every one of us, all the time.

At the end of my one year living without my money, I realised God gave me far more than I would have ever given myself. I found myself in the most beautiful places, surrounded by the most beautiful people. During that year I travelled to Israel, Bali, France, Spain, Holland, Scotland and America. Money just kept coming to me without me even asking, which in itself was a miracle. I also found it so much easier to give money away to those who needed it more than I did, even though I didn't know when or how I'd receive more for myself to live on.

Sometimes, when dining out with others, I'd be asked to share about my journey and the miracles I'd received. Some were so moved by my story they would insist on paying for my meal. Others would just come up to me and put money in my hand because they admired what I was doing. It was so beautiful; every one of these amazingly kind and generous people were, I believe, sent to me by God.

I realised we are *all* surrounded by God's loving angels, and they'll reveal themselves to us when we trust in that higher consciousness so many of us call God. I now know from my own experience that if we just trust, we'll always be okay. I'm truly grateful that, with the help of my two spiritual teachers, I chose to answer the call and trust my original message. It was an amazing year filled with *so* much love.

I'm certain the message I received to live a year as if I had no money was from a higher, loving Source. It brought me freedom from many fears, *especially* about how I'd survive if I lost all my money! It also showed me that people are genuinely kind and helped me trust in the love of human beings rather than believing no one would want to help me. Once again, I got to experience that:

Love Is Truth and Love WILL Set You Free!

Chapter 8

Healing Cancer ... And So Much More!

A few years ago, a very small spot appeared just above my lip that looked a little bit like a blackhead. It was so small to start with, it was practically unnoticeable. After about two years, it started to form a flaky, dry skin over the area that would then drop off, leaving a red spot. Because it started to become noticeable, I decided to see a skin specialist.

I was in a really good mood during that first appointment because I'd attended a laughter workshop the day before, which took me out of seriousness, worry and fear. I told the doctor the history of the spot. Without even looking at it, he said, 'I can see from just looking at you that you have skin damage all over.' Then he looked at my back and asked me to roll up my sleeve, saying, 'As I thought ... skin damage everywhere! Your body should look just like the skin on your bottom.' I asked him if he was referring to my freckles, to which he replied, 'yes'. I giggled to myself, knowing my bottom was also covered in freckles and pictured myself bending over, revealing to him that he was, in fact, mistaken.

Eventually, the doctor looked at the spot on my lip and said it was definitely cancer, and it should be removed quickly. He didn't mention at this point it wasn't a fatal type of cancer, so I was feeling quite shocked at his diagnosis. I was also still amused at his serious manner. I asked him if the procedure would leave a scar, and he replied, 'You can lose half your lip before you need to worry.' I said with a smile, 'All doom and gloom then. It's a good thing I'm not worried about death!' Only then did he say it wasn't a fatal form of cancer, but it would 'spread all over' my face if I didn't have it removed. Then he suggested I go into the treatment room and have some of it cut out to be tested. As I was leaving, he said, 'It's plenty of sun block for you, young lady, and keep your clothes on in the future.'

By this time, I was trying really hard not to laugh; his serious and insensitive manner was so outrageous. He never looked me in the eye once during the whole consultation. When the door closed, I burst out laughing, sensing immediately I shouldn't proceed with the treatment. Thank goodness for the laughter workshop the day before!

I'd just read a book entitled *The Healing Effects of Sunlight* by Andreas Moritz, which helped me recognize the doctor wasn't coming from a holistic place; indeed, he was making statements that weren't even factual about my freckly skin. I told the nurse I wanted to go home and think about it before going ahead with their suggested procedure.

The experience with this 'specialist' felt like a comedy sketch. In hindsight, it was perfect: If the whole thing hadn't felt so bizarre, I might have proceeded with his advice. Instead, I looked into some alternative treatments. I'd been told that cannabis oil was very effective for skin cancers. I spent two weeks investigating this possibility but discovered it was illegal in the UK. I instinctively knew that I'd be able to find something else that would work. I felt (surprisingly) very calm about it all.

I discovered that someone I was doing an online healing course with was a certified doctor in orthodox medicine but had become an alternative holistic practitioner. He recommended a cream called Curaderm that was both effective and legal. He also advised that I sit quietly, light a candle, breathe and ask the cancer what it was trying to communicate to me. He suggested I continue this every day until I received a clear answer. He suggested I make friends with the cancer, asking it to reveal itself to me in the form of a being or animal. I believe he suggested this so it could communicate with me better.

I felt amazed at the synchronistic events that were unfolding. So, I ordered the cream and began the doctor's suggested daily inquiry.

The first time I connected with the cancer, I saw an imp-like, female being who was sneaky, but also attractive and mischievous. The message I received was about not being honest, but at the time, I didn't know what it was referring to. Two days later, the cream arrived, and I began the treatment.

The cream worked by eating away at the cancer, pulling it out at its root. The pain was intense; it burned immensely when applied. The ingredients of the cream were derived from eggplant (Aborigines discovered that when their cows developed skin problems, they healed themselves by rubbing up against eggplant plants). I was aware that using the cream would be a long process – to achieve 100% success, it had to be used for a minimum of eight weeks, but it could take up to 12. The cream had to be applied at least twice a day and had to be covered so it wouldn't dry out. I learned that if the cream was applied more often, the cancer would clear up faster.

I continued to do the inquiry process along with the application of the cream, applying it about five times a day. I went in and out of fear as I watched the wound grow bigger and bigger, until it had spread right across the top left side of my lip. The first time I went out with microtape on my lip, I felt self-conscious, thinking everyone was looking at me. Sometimes, I'd cry and get *so* angry at God because the cancer was right on my face. It was so prominent. At times, the fear became very intense – I was so afraid the cancer would spread even further across my face.

After only four weeks, the cancer was almost healed. Then, almost overnight, it became red and even larger and more painful when the cream was applied. I was frantic. The people I ordered it from reassured me that it was quite normal for the pain to increase as the cream burnt into the cancer; this was due to it reaching the nerves as it penetrated deeper.

I'd wake up every morning hoping it looked better. But every morning, it was only getting bigger and even more painful. I sank further into despair while still putting on a smile for everyone, hiding my fear. One morning, feeling desperate and alone, I began to cry. I lay down and began to breathe, asking for guidance from Yeshua (Jesus).

Immediately, I saw myself in a past life as a woman in a cage. I had a skin disease all over (including my face), and I was being teased and poked with sticks by other women. I felt intense grief and loneliness, believing I was completely unlovable.

The cancer on my lip now was bringing up very similar feelings of fear. I began to understand why, in this lifetime, image had always meant so much to me: I believed if I didn't look good, I'd be worthless, unlovable and alone. It made so much sense why this cancer was bringing up so much terror in me. Now, I see that having the cancer displayed so prominently on my face was surfacing all my fears and heightening all my ego patterns.

But while I gained some comfort from seeing *why* I was feeling this way, I still felt consumed by fear.

At the same time I was trying to treat my cancer, a desire arose to attend a workshop retreat happening in Bali. My ego kept coming up with all kinds of justifications for not going: It would be irresponsible to go whilst the wound on my lip was so raw and painful, etc. Still, I sent an email asking if it was too late to enrol and received an immediate answer that there were still spaces available. So, I booked a flight that day to leave three weeks later.

During the following weeks, the cancer wound got bigger and increasingly more painful. By the time I left to go to Bali,

I felt great despair and fear. When I reached the ashram where the workshop was being held, the despair was written all over my face; I could no longer keep on the false smile. I cried when people hugged me from the relief of letting that go.

During the workshop, we explored different ego personas using the nine Enneagram types. I discovered we each have a certain pattern that dominates our thoughts, keeping us feeling separate from our Source / God and inner peace. Here, I experienced another miracle: If it hadn't been for the cancer on my lip, I would never have been able to discover a deep pattern in me that I hadn't seen before.

I'd always found it difficult to be around people who felt sorry for themselves, believing *I* wasn't like that at all. I'd always picked myself up, put a brave smile on my face and hid how bad I was feeling inside. I discovered this was only a type of mask I'd mastered wearing since I was very young: I'd believed it was more important to *look* good to others than to express honestly how badly I felt. I'd cover up my feelings with a smile while, deep down, I actually felt victimized by life and God. I'd deceived myself (and others) by covering up what was really going on for me ... and had no idea this was dishonest!

I was able to see all the different times in my life where I'd used this strategy to cope. This amazing discovery came after I realised that my despair about the cancer was coming from a deep feeling of being a victim. I had lots of thoughts going around in my head regarding the cancer, like, 'Why is this happening to me?' and, 'Why is God doing this to me?' I'd been looking at everyone I met with anger that I was the only one who had this going on. Why did it have to be right on my face? I constantly questioned how God could do this to me after all I had done to grow spiritually and become a better person. It felt like I was being punished for something!

When I finally became aware of my thoughts, I saw clearly where I'd played the victim throughout my whole life. I saw a time as a child when I wished I had other parents than my own. I saw how often I'd felt depressed growing up and cried in secret when things seemed to be going wrong for me. I was able to see so many ways that I'd felt like a victim ... which is, of course, the same as feeling sorry for myself – the very thing I couldn't stand in others!

At this point, all I could do was laugh at myself. It started to bubble up inside me and, despite the pain on my lip, I laughed as much as I could. For the first time, I felt *gratitude* for the cancer: It revealed this lifelong pattern to me! If it hadn't been *right in my face,* I never would have discovered it.

I also realised it's impossible to feel gratitude and victimization at the same time. Victimhood is a guaranteed way to take us out of peace and into hopelessness. I've heard it said that one of the most common mental addictions is the one to victimhood. Most people aren't even aware they have it!

After this newly discovered realisation, I awoke at three in the morning and couldn't get back to sleep, so I pulled back the mosquito net over my bed and looked at the beautiful stars shining brightly in the sky. I felt a huge sense of relief, despite still having a huge, open wound above my lip. I closed my eyes. Suddenly, something wet and cold landed right on my lip! I jumped up and knocked it off, only to discover it was a frog! It had landed right on the cancer wound, not touching any other part of me. What were the odds it would land right on the cancer?

In the morning, I told my roommate what had happened, and she told me she'd also woken up at three because she'd felt Yeshua's presence so strongly in the room. I felt I'd been kissed by Yeshua! The next day, someone in the workshop exclaimed, 'It's definitely going to heal now!'

Immediately after this, the cancer started to disappear. Within two-and-a-half-weeks it was completely gone. No scar.

I now know the cancer came to show me an unhealthy pattern unconsciously running me for most of my life, and that if I had just allowed it to be cut out (as recommended by the skin specialist), I'd never have discovered it. Now, I'm so much more aware when my mind starts to convince me I'm a victim, and I do my best to catch it as quickly as possible. When I do, and change my thinking, wow! It saves me from so much suffering!

I can also see why, when I spoke to the cancer at the very beginning of this journey, it appeared to me as an imp-like being who was sneaky, mischievous and dishonest. The pattern had caused *me* to be dishonest and sneaky about my true feelings. The strategy of putting on a smile was–also mischievous (although at that point it was an unconscious behaviour). I was in total denial of it, believing I *definitely* wasn't someone who felt sorry for myself (just because I wasn't doing it openly)!

I realised I probably had many more unconscious beliefs and thoughts that weren't serving me. My journey was to discover these destructive patterns of denial, so I could act from Love, not fear, and to be able to get so truthful with myself that the ego had no chance of winning. Through this journey, I discovered once again that:

Love is Truth and Love Will Set You Free!

Chapter 9

Healing With My Son, Part One

Have you ever struggled to know what to do with a difficult teenager? The miracle I'm about to share with you has the potential to return you to peace. If you find yourself in a situation with a child of *any* age that seems hopeless to resolve, maybe the following experience will help you shift your perception from fear to Love.

When my son was about 14 years old, I had a great deal of trouble getting him out of bed in the morning for school. I was a single parent at the time, raising three boys. It eventually got so bad that, almost every morning, I couldn't get him up at all and had to leave him in bed to get my other two sons to school on time. My 14-year-old would finally get up around 11am and get to school very late. I started receiving letters from teachers threatening me with fines if he didn't improve his attendance.

I asked for advice from everyone. His father, who wasn't living with us at the time, told me I was too 'soft' with him, and my parents were also saying I wasn't strict enough. Desperate, I tried some of their advice, which only ended up making things worse. One suggestion was to throw cold water over him to get him out of bed in the morning. I *really* didn't want to do this, and as you can imagine, it did *not* go well. He screamed and swore at me and still wouldn't get up. Someone else suggested pulling the covers off him. This also didn't end well: Pulling the covers off a 14-and-a-half-year-old boy who wasn't wearing pyjamas was humiliating for both of us and made him even more angry.

Each time I tried to force him out of bed using different methods suggested by others, the result was huge drama. He became insanely angry, and I ended up increasingly upset and depressed about the whole thing. It was a horrible way to start the day, for all of us.

The final straw came one morning when he shouted and screamed so many hurtful accusations at me that I lost my temper and started to hit him. I cried out, 'I hate you! I hate you!' All he did in response was laugh. I'd never hit my children before; I didn't agree with responding in that way. I ran out of his room, crying, feeling immensely ashamed. I cried out to God, 'Please show me another way.'

Immediately, a question entered my mind:

'If you didn't have the school sending threatening letters, and if you didn't have your ex-husband and parents giving you their advice, what would you do?' Then, another question arose: 'What if you didn't believe he would never get a job or survive if he got bad grades or didn't pass his exams?'

In that moment, I realised these were the exact fears causing so much anxiety within me. As I contemplated how I would respond to my son *without* these beliefs, all the fear I had around these issues suddenly disappeared. I decided there was no way I could possibly know with one hundred percent certainty that my beliefs were true; I needed to put my trust fully in God and *not* in society's rules or ideas. I was going to trust it would all work out and I could stop trying to change my son and the situation.

The next morning, I went into my son's room feeling only love in my heart for him. I put the light on and said, 'Time to get up for school!' Then I left, happily waking up my other two sons and continuing making breakfast. This time, I really was in a good mood, with no expectations that my 14-year-old *had* to get up. I went to his bedroom again before leaving and said very kindly to him, 'If you're coming with us, we'll be leaving in ten minutes.' When he still didn't emerge, I went back upstairs, turned his light back off, and said very cheerfully, 'See you later!'

Wow! What a difference! No stress! The judgement and blame I'd heaped on my son was no longer present. Instead, a tremendous love returned for him that I'd lost touch with during all those months of struggle.

Of course, my two other sons couldn't understand why I was letting their 14-year-old brother get away with it without a fight. I reassured them that all was well, and in a joyful, non-judging tone of voice, said it was his choice if he didn't want to go to school and pass his exams.

When I got home, my son was still in bed. He got up around 11am, and I welcomed him with a big, loving smile and asked him if he wanted to join me for a late breakfast. He looked bemused but said yes. I never mentioned anything about him not getting up for school, and we had a few nice exchanges. This continued for about a week.

Slowly, he began getting up earlier and earlier and going to school. He didn't always get up early enough to arrive on time, but his attendance improved tremendously. He passed most of his final exams and now has a great career earning very good money.

Before I questioned my thoughts, I'd been driven by my own fear and listening to the advice of other fearful beings. As soon as I stopped following these fearful ways of thinking (which were common 'rules' of the educational system and society in general), I could hear my heart speak to me. It took me becoming totally exasperated with my son to finally surrender to another way.

To me, listening to my heart was allowing God to speak to me. I received the answers to all my questions, which brought me out of fear and deeply into Love.

It's sometimes very difficult to find a peaceful solution to a stressful situation because fear is literally blocking you from receiving Love's guidance. It takes courage, and trust, to go against what everyone else is telling you – *especially* if it comes from firmly established societal beliefs.

We call God an almighty, loving force we can connect to any time we desire. When we ask for God's help in *any* situation, we're literally opening ourselves up to Love's way.

God's awesome guidance will bring you a profound peace you never thought possible!

For Love is Truth and Love Will Set You Free!

Chapter 10

Healing With My Son, Part Two

More than anything else in life, I wanted to be a really good mother. I've been blessed with three amazing sons, and they're all completely different. One of my sons was not as tidy as the other two; going through the teenage years proved to be quite challenging.

Can you relate to having to ask your children over and over again to do something and feeling totally exasperated when they just won't do it? I've come to believe it's the story we make up about *why* they're not behaving as we want them to that causes us the most heartache.

Here's how I came to see that I needed to look at *my* beliefs to bring peace to a very frustrating scenario.

~

Every day after showering, my teenage son would leave his wet towel on his bed and his clothes and socks on the floor. He never made his bed, and the clothes I'd ironed for him and put away so nicely in his drawers would be flung all over the floor. I asked him constantly to not do these things, but nothing I said changed his behaviour. I felt angry and distraught, not understanding how he could do this to me when he knew how upset it made me. It was a very unpleasant way to start the day, for both of us. The situation also affected my other sons – they weren't experiencing the best of me, as arguments with their brother would ensue every morning.

During this difficult time with my son, I was reading a book by Byron Katie entitled *Loving What Is*. At a very low time in her own life, this amazing woman learnt to question all her fearful beliefs, discovering they weren't actually true. With radical self-honesty and love for herself, she discovered that, in any situation, she could choose to return to peace, simply by questioning her thoughts.

I continued feeling awful and completely overwhelmed with despair over the situation with my messy teenage son. I remembered Katie sharing one of her own experiences with her child not picking up their socks and how she'd changed her whole thought system around it by questioning her beliefs around *why* her child *should* clean up after themselves. I began to question my own beliefs around why my son wasn't doing what I asked him to do.

I saw that under my anger lay a deep sadness; I believed he couldn't possibly care about me if he didn't do what I asked. I also recognised I believed he *must* be doing it deliberately. If this were true, I assumed I must've done something wrong as a mother to cause him to treat me this way. Why didn't he love me? This belief led to yet another fear arising within me: If I didn't get him to change these untidy habits now, he'd never be able to maintain a happy relationship with a future partner. And that would make *me* a bad mother ... so I had to persist in getting him to do as I asked!

I saw how my mind was simply spiralling down into negativity and fear of the future. No wonder I was feeling so awful about myself and my son – I actually believed all these thoughts! I saw very clearly that in this state of mind, I'd completely forgotten how much I loved him. So, I chose in that moment to question *all* my beliefs and, one by one, I asked myself if they were *really* true.

This changed everything! I saw that I could *choose* another thought that was much more loving towards myself *and* my son and that was actually truer. I realised it was just not important to my son to have a tidy room, even though it was *very* important to *me*. He also had different priorities than I did in general, and *I* was the one making his behaviour mean he didn't care about me.

I saw that believing he didn't care or love me led me to accusing him of deliberately trying to hurt me. With self-inquiry, I realised how unloving and judgemental I'd become towards him. Then, I questioned the beliefs I had about how his future would be if I didn't force him to change. By questioning these beliefs, I realised that by nagging him, I'd probably only make him worse. Then it dawned on me: If my son was going to be untidy in the future, he'd probably be that way regardless of anything I said or did now.

I asked myself if I could allow him the choice to be untidy and to experience the consequences that might occur for him in the future if he continued to be so. After all, months of nagging him to be tidier clearly didn't work. Someone once said to me, 'If you ask someone to do something once, then that's understandable, but if you keep on asking them, then you are being controlling.' But if someone continues to do something you *can't* control, it's time to focus on what you *can* control ... and the only thing we can really control are our own thoughts, actions and reactions.

Another insight occurred when I realised that if it meant so much to me to have his bed made, the socks picked up and the wet towel hung up to dry, then I could do it myself! The most important thing of all was that I do it with love. I could also choose to stop thinking about the future and predicting the worst-case scenario and, instead, just trust all would be well. I could choose Love over fear and find ways to love my son instead of judging him.

Of course, this way of thinking goes against what most of us were brought up to believe and the way society tells us to react when our kids don't do what we say. We're told this kind of behaviour spoils them and we must make them do things our way – even if it means constant fighting and arguing. We're taught to worry about the future, but by doing so we miss out on the present moment.

It's helpful to ask ourselves at times like these, *How important is this?* Of course, if your children (or anyone else) are acting in a way that's genuinely harmful towards you, the loving answer may be to put distance between you. Those decisions take a lot more courage than just staying in harmful situations.

We live in a society where judging one another seems normal; when we do so, we lose sight of what Love is. We say we 'love' our children, but often end up hating them because we get lost in our fears and judgements about them – and about ourselves as parents. Without realising it, we may find ourselves behaving worse than our children do. This all happens unconsciously until we take the time to question our own thinking.

When I questioned my thoughts about my son and saw the beliefs running me, love and understanding returned. I became joyful and peaceful again in the mornings. My other sons' lives improved tremendously because they didn't have to suffer my anger and sadness every day or hear me venting my judgements towards their brother.

Another miracle came from my newfound peace quite organically: I saw a way to resolve yet another problem with my untidy son.

My eldest son was very particular about his shirts being ironed to his standard and started to complain about my ironing skills. He'd often iron his clothes again because he was much better at it than I was. This didn't upset me too much; it was good to see him becoming more responsible.

But I still had a huge pile of un-ironed clothes overflowing in a basket in the corner of my kitchen. It never seemed to decrease in size, which was extremely depressing.

I decided instead of ironing our clean, dry clothes, I'd simply fold them neatly and put them away in our respective drawers, to be ironed when we needed them. I informed my two eldest sons they were now capable enough to iron their own clothes. The endless pile of ironing completely disappeared, and I never had to look at it again.

My eldest son accepted this new arrangement very quickly. My middle son didn't care enough to iron his clothes at all, choosing to wear his clothes un-ironed and creased. This was challenging for me at first. What would people think about me allowing my son to go out looking that way? But somehow in my newfound peace I became completely accepting of both his choice and mine, and my resentment toward his behaviour of throwing the clothes I'd so carefully ironed and put away in his drawers disappeared.

I've learnt there's always a way to bring peace and love to a situation instead of getting consumed with judgement and fear. It does, however, take a lot of self-honesty and willingness to think in new ways and be able to let go of our previous beliefs and conditionings.

There's a saying that the greatest form of insanity is doing the same thing over and over again while expecting a different result. Honest self-inquiry, coupled with the willingness to find a loving answer, is the most powerful way to profoundly improve our lives.

Love is Honesty and Love Will Set You Free!

Chapter 11

Healing with The Headmistress

W hen my two eldest sons were in primary school, I had to sign up for financial support from the government due to a separation from my partner, who'd been financially providing for us. The amount I was given was barely enough to survive on, but one thing I was entitled to was free school meals for my sons.

The local school my sons attended was run by a wealthy family who owned the estate it was built on. Most of the children attending the school were also from wealthy families. The headmistress was a well-spoken woman who, at the time, I regarded as cold-hearted. I was intimidated by her most of the time. When she spoke to me, she addressed me as if she were talking to one of her child students, and so having to ask for free school meals was very humiliating.

I made an appointment to see her, and she told me I had to fill out a form but didn't tell me it would need to be returned by a certain date for my sons to qualify for free meals that week. She informed me she didn't have the form so would have to get one for me. After a few days, I saw her on the playground and asked her again for the form, but she still didn't have it. I eventually received it a few days later. I completed the form, but when I handed it back to her, she said we weren't entitled to free school meals for that week because it hadn't been turned in on time. I explained to her the reason I'd missed the date required was because she delayed getting the form to me. I stressed I *needed* the free school meals to start that week and asked her if there was anything she could do? She was dismissive and wouldn't take responsibility for the fact she didn't get the form to me on time. I was fuming!

I left feeling unsupported and deeply upset. I went home and cried. I was already feeling so much fear around my financial situation – I had no idea at the time how I was going to survive without my partner's support and if I was going to be able to keep a roof over our heads. The headmistress's uncaring attitude took me deeper into despair. I began to hate this woman! With so much anger and resentment inside me, I thought I must try again to get her to take responsibility for the form not being handed in on time.

I made another appointment to speak with the headmistress. I arrived prepared for an argument, knowing what her attitude had previously been. My guard was up. I began to ask again if she would reconsider her decision, but she ordered me to sit down, refusing to speak with me while I was standing up. I told her to not treat me like one of her students. The whole conversation went from bad to worse. I left feeling immense anger and even more hatred for this woman. For weeks, I allowed the feelings to fester and affect my life. I told everyone I could how heartless and disrespectful the headmistress was towards me, especially since she knew about my situation. I felt like a victim. It was literally destroying my health, my strength, and my will to go on.

At the time, I was attending a Twelve Step program called Al-Anon, a program for people who have family or friends struggling with addiction to alcohol.* Part of the Twelve Step program taught me to take responsibility for our own anger and resentments. This takes tremendous self-honesty (and a very patient and loving sponsor to guide you in the process. My sponsor needed to be very direct with me because I argued for my right to be right with many of my resentments).

The deepest resentment I held at the time was the one with the headmistress. I was encouraged to write down all the ways I was judging her – all the things I was thinking about her (like being so selfish and not even caring about my situation). The list was long, and I felt very justified in my accusations. But what my sponsor pointed out to me was that, in my fearful state about money and deep need to be right, I'd forgotten to consider *why* she may have acted the way she did.

I hadn't stopped to question what the headmistress may

---

* Please see 'Recommended Resources' for a list of Twelve Step programs.

have been protecting or fearing within herself. What was *she* going through? Was she overworked or feeling pressured? I also came to see that I'd approached her from the start with preconceived ideas that she was harsh and cold-hearted. Every time I met with her, I *expected* there would be resistance and conflict. I didn't enter conversations with her lovingly, calmly and with good thoughts about her at all. Instead, I went in with anger and judgement. It was a setup for disaster!

My sponsor pointed out that we pick up on the energy and thoughts of each other, even if we're not consciously aware of it. It took quite some time for this new notion to break through my self-righteousness, but when it finally *did* sink in, I could clearly see my part in the situation. I owned that I'd acted out of fear and been selfish, self-seeking and dishonest. The fear I felt around my financial situation had clouded my judgement; I'd only been thinking of my own problems, with no consideration of her at all. I was driven by fear going into that second meeting, needing to get my own way no matter what.

Amazingly, I felt overwhelming relief with these realizations; I no longer felt like a victim. My sponsor pointed out to me this *didn't* mean that the headmistress hadn't reacted unsympathetically towards me, only that my fear caused me to act in the same way towards her.

One of the next steps, after seeing my resentments, was to make amends to this woman for the energy in which I'd approached the whole situation. This terrified me, but I knew that to grow spiritually and be truly free of my emotional pain, it was something I needed to do. While there were other people I wanted to make amends with, the headmistress was at the top of my list; it was the thought of making amends to her, specifically, that brought up the most fear. She was also the person I held the most anger and resentment towards at the time.

To make my amends, I made yet another appointment with the headmistress, knowing she was probably expecting me to arrive with the same confronting energy as before. As I started walking towards her office, my mind screamed out, *Don't do this! She'll just tell you to go away and that she's not interested in what you have to say!* I was terrified of being totally humiliated. My mind raced with fear as I imagined this and dozens of other scenarios. But I remembered my sponsor's words: I was doing this for my own healing, and it didn't really matter *how* she reacted. All that mattered was that I have the courage to make amends despite my fears. Then, I could walk away, knowing I'd done the right thing. How she might react was out of my control.

When making amends, it's suggested to write down *exactly* what you want to say. It was important to make my words clear and clean without mentioning a single thing about what I thought she'd done to me – that would cancel out any amends I was intending to make. If we say, 'I'm sorry, but ...', what we're actually saying is, 'I was totally justified in my actions and am not really sorry at all.'

This is the speech I was given by my sponsor to deliver to anyone I desired to make amends with:

I am trying to enlarge upon my spiritual life, which requires that I do my utmost to straighten out the past. Due to issues in my life I have not dealt with, I have been selfish, self-seeking, dishonest and anxious. This has been a fault in me, and I regret this. In the future, I will listen to what you have to say and see where your experience can be of benefit to me. I will be available and supportive to you whenever I can.

This speech prevents us from going into story and justification, owning our own part and the energy we've been acting from. (It also takes even more courage to say it in this format).

With this prepared speech in hand, I knocked on the headmistress's office door, took a deep breath and entered. I noticed she greeted me in a posture of defensiveness and that she appeared quite stern. I calmly sat down and said in a very peaceful voice, 'I have something I would like to say to you.' She looked nervous but allowed me to go ahead. I began to tremble, and the piece of paper started to shake in my hands as I began to read. After reading the first sentence, I could hardly breath and had to pause. My lip began to quiver, and tears filled my eyes. I was too afraid at that point to look up, so I took a deep breath and continued.

How I got through that speech without crying my eyes out I'll never know. But as I got to the end, I knew I *had* to look up and face her. I was terrified and began to shake again, but as I looked up, to my complete and utter astonishment, she slowly removed her glasses and wiped away a tear.

My whole perception of her changed in an instant. The woman sitting before me wasn't 'heartless'. Instead, she was calm and sensitive. She said, 'Wow, that must have taken a lot of courage to come here and say that to me. Please tell me, what spiritual path you are following?' I told her about the

Twelve Step program and that the reason I was in it was because someone in my family was an alcoholic. She immediately opened up, telling me she, too, had someone in her family who was struggling with addiction. We had a beautiful conversation that ended with her thanking me again for being so kind and brave. I left that day feeling elated. I experienced a freedom and joy that couldn't be put into words. I also felt a true, loving connection with her for the first time. It was a moment I'll never forget.

I still had to pay for that week's school lunches, but it just didn't matter to me anymore. The whole experience was so meaningful that I felt it was well worth the cost of a week's lunch money. From that day forward, I felt the headmistress had a respect for me that she hadn't had before. When difficult situations arose after that, she always spoke to me very kindly. I felt she really trusted me.

I learnt that it was only my *perception* of her and the situation that was the cause of my pain. By being willing to own this, I was set free.

I continue to use the Twelve Steps to this day to help me see things differently when I lose my peace. Most of us need to suffer a while before being willing to lovingly look at *our* part in difficult or painful situations, but:

When We Choose Love it Will Always Set Us Free!

Chapter 12

The Booming Voice

Have you ever experienced something beyond this world and immediately told yourself you must be imagining it? You dismiss what you've just seen, felt or heard. This is usually ego overriding Truth. The booming voice I experienced in this story was certainly one of those times, but despite the ego's attempt to dismiss it, I didn't allow the mind to overpower what I *knew* I'd experienced.

One morning, I was reading a book entitled *A Course in Miracles*. It contains profound teachings from Jesus, scribed by a woman named Helen Schucman. I'd been absorbing Jesus's loving messages through this book for a number of years and was dedicated to reading at least one passage every morning before getting out of bed. On this particular morning, the chapter I was reading was all about 'special relationship'; in particular, the romantic love relationship. As I absorbed the words, a huge insight washed over me, a profound realisation felt throughout my entire being. It came with a feeling of lightness and excitement as I realised how I'd been operating from ego in my own romantic relationships: Up to this point, my relationships hadn't been working out, and I couldn't understand why. It became so clear to me that what I was believing and thinking was creating disfunction in my relationships.

Suddenly, I heard a powerful, booming voice say, 'BE WANTED'! It felt like it was mainly coming from behind me, yet it surrounded me from every direction, too. I felt the words reverberate through the left side of my head, leaving a tingling sensation inside my skull. It felt so weird, but I wasn't afraid. I tapped and shook my head a few times and, despite the remaining tingling, my mind still tried to dismiss it!

The voice had a power and loudness that felt masculine, but the loving essence it contained was so profound it also felt feminine. The words were delivered with a unique tone and clarity unlike any voice of this world. I'd never heard so much power in a voice that also contained so much love!

After accepting I really *did* hear these words, I heard a softer voice in my head say, 'Can you really deny what you just heard even while the left side of your head is still tingling?' I looked behind me for the source of the voice. Of course, there was only my bedroom wall and headboard. As I sat there, stunned, I asked the voice, 'What does that mean, "be wanted?'" Before I'd even finished asking the question, the reply came, this time from within me. In a quiet, loving tone of voice, it said, 'Be wanted by God, not by a man.'

Immediately, my heart sank. All my life, I'd wanted to be wanted by a man. I'd longed to find that one special love that would fulfil me, so hearing these words shattered my hopes and dreams. I desperately wanted to feel and know God's Love, but I didn't want to give up on my fantasy of a romantic love relationship. I thought wanting God *more* than I wanted a man was never going to be as fulfilling. I thought, *I can't kiss and make love to God, I can't even see God, so how can I possibly desire being wanted by God* more *than I desire being wanted by a man?* I so longed to be held in the arms of a man who adored me and wanted to make me his number one focus, a man who would take care of me and take away all my worries. I was incredibly resistant to this profound communication. Obviously, I just wasn't ready to hear or believe that *God* would bring me more happiness than a man.

Now, God has a great sense of humour and an infinite amount of patience. A few years later, I was in a relationship with a man I adored, because he wanted me so much. I truly felt like I was his number one priority. I thought (at first) he was the answer to my dreams. He'd clean the house and look for ways to please me. He was a great lover; the sex was out of this world. Our chemistry was so powerful, we couldn't keep our hands off each other.

After only a few weeks of living together, I became very

sore from making love too often and for too long. I told my partner my body just couldn't handle it, so we needed to slow it down a bit. Unfortunately, he took this to mean I was rejecting him (despite the fact we were making love for hours at a time at least four times a day). No matter how many times I tried to explain it wasn't *him* I was rejecting, he wouldn't accept my reasoning. I was unable to console him, which led to our first intense argument.

Soon after, I noticed I often couldn't find my handbag or clothes where I'd left them. I discovered my partner was keeping them so he could come to my rescue when I couldn't find them. One day, as we were heading out, I spent about 15 minutes looking for my phone and keys, not understanding why they weren't where I was *sure* I'd left them. Eventually, I asked him if he'd seen them, and he handed them over, saying, 'I collected them for you so we'd be ready on time.' I was furious! I started to doubt my own sanity when things weren't where I'd left them. Another time, he rearranged the clothes in my drawers without asking me. When I asked him to stop doing these things, he got very defensive and refused to see my perspective. Instead, he'd say I wasn't 'tidy enough' and that I *needed* him to take care of me. I started to feel afraid to say anything, fearing he'd turn it around on me by putting me down (like he did when he told me it was my fault I 'couldn't remember' where I'd put things).

The relationship didn't last long; my partner wasn't able to see his 'helpfulness' was actually suffocating me. It was like my life force was ebbing away. It was only after the relationship ended that I remembered what that Booming

Voice had said. I realised God had sent me my wish: a man totally focused on trying to please me, a man who needed to make love to me for most of the day just so I could feel wanted. When I realised this, I laughed and laughed and felt God's love for me more than ever.

I knew then I would never be fulfilled by a man. By granting me this experience, God showed me my egoic wish was never going to bring me the connection and love I sought. It was time for me to focus on my connection to God *first*. I knew this didn't mean I had to become a nun, or never be in a relationship with a man again, but that *no* relationship would ever work if I was looking for a partner to complete me or fulfil me in any way! Only accepting God's love for me – and loving myself! – could do that. I needed to turn back to the Love that created me and fill myself up with *that* love first. Wanting God to have *all* of me was the only way I could become the Love I was meant to be.

The Booming Voice I heard that day was pure wisdom and truth. As the Sufi poet Rumi says, 'What you seek is seeking you.' If I truly wanted to experience myself as the Love I am, and be *truly* capable of loving another, my first focus and desire must be for God's love for me. This made the statement from the Bible ring true: 'Seek ye first the kingdom of heaven and all else shall be added unto you.' I'd mistakenly believed I had to love God first *before* I could accept God's love for me; many spiritual teachings I'd studied told me so. But what was *more* true was that I had to desire to be wanted by *God* just as much as I desired to be wanted by a man.

This profound shift in thinking explained why I hadn't been feeling connected to my Creator (the one I call God). I realised it'd been so hard to love *anyone* when I wasn't accepting how much God was *already* loving me! This is the only love that brings us true joy and fulfilment. Otherwise, we're empty, trying to fill ourselves with love from another, fooling ourselves that we're being loving instead of needy.

I find it difficult to explain to those who don't believe in God (or who haven't had this kind of experience) how wonderful it truly feels to know how much we *are* loved *right now* – no matter what we have or haven't done. God just loves us unconditionally, all the time.

Some of us can't accept God is loving in *all* situations, because we don't realise *every* situation is a chance for us to see exactly where God is trying to help us. Each seeming disaster actually creates an opportunity for us to expand our awareness of love even more deeply, redirecting us towards something greater.

We have a choice: lose faith in a loving God or ask God to help us see the gift in what's occurring. We can choose to get angry or resentful about our situation, or we can choose to become more loving, trusting and accepting of God's plan for us.

I've come to know God doesn't punish us, for Love would never do that (and God is Love). Every adversity is an opportunity for us to choose another way. To turn back to our creator and ask to see the situation through the eyes of Love. For Love is our true Divine nature not fear: And that is why:

Love Is Truth and Love Will Set You Free.

Chapter 13

All Resisted Darkness and Fear is Just Play

One afternoon, I was sitting in my friend's kitchen, feeling distraught about yet another one of my intimate relationships ending. My friend, who knew about breath work, asked if I wanted to breathe into and explore the sadness I was feeling. I agreed. I felt into the grief and started to go into a very dark place. As I went deeper into the experience, it became even more terrifying. I really didn't want to continue. I saw images of a long, ghostly white face, like a mask you wear at Halloween. It started to become almost unbearable, as it was bringing up more and more fear. As I breathed in even more deeply, it intensified, and I burst into tears. I then became aware that the images were representing fear itself.

A deep sadness and grief arose as I went into the fear. Then a picture of my ex-boyfriend in the arms of another woman flashed before my eyes. Only two days after we split up, this image appeared on Facebook. I realised the grief I was experiencing was because I felt I was a total failure. I'd decided he couldn't have felt much love for me because he'd moved on so quickly. This seemed to confirm my belief that I just wasn't good enough.

I stayed with the feelings even though every part of me did *not* want to go there in case I discovered I was, in fact, really worthless, and fundamentally flawed. This showed me that the true underlying fear wasn't even about the relationship ending, but me maybe discovering I truly was unlovable.

As I kept breathing, I moved deeper and deeper towards the images and feelings of terror. Suddenly all the horrible, ghostly images turned into nursery rhyme characters. One was like *The Owl and the Pussycat,* with a dancing spoon wearing a happy smile. Everything instantaneously turned into play!

Then I saw that beyond the playful, happy characters was a beautiful lake and stunning, luscious meadow with the sun shining brightly above it. An image appeared of Jesus with his arms stretched out towards me saying, 'Now will you let me love you?'

I cried with joy, realising that everything *other* than joy and love was an illusion: It was just my own mind making things up through the lens of my fear. Love was there all along, waiting for me to claim it! Wow! I was awe struck and felt amazing for the rest of the day.

Slowly, over time, I forgot about this powerful vision, but I know in my heart that it was real and true. The vision showed me I had nothing to fear – all the darkness and fearful beliefs about myself were just stories I made up. Life is but a play! It isn't good or bad, just stories we believe in.

Witnessing Jesus with his arms stretched out towards me, asking me to allow him to love me, was the most wonderful feeling of freedom and love I've ever felt. Jesus showed me the Truth about darkness and fear, and I laughed to see how ridiculous it was. Once again, the Truth was revealed as Love and:

Love Will Set You Free!

Chapter 14

Finding Freedom from Unhealthy Relationships

For almost all my life, I attracted difficult intimate relationships with men. I was in love with all my partners, but I like to say I stayed with many of them way past the relationship's 'sell-by' date. If you've ever remained in a tumultuous relationship knowing deep down it wasn't working, maybe you can relate. Many of us do this because we're desperately hanging on to a hope that *someday* it will change.

When things started to fall apart in my relationships, I'd remind myself how it was when we first fell in love and how attentive my partner had been towards me. I was constantly trying to hold on to the way it *had* been rather than admitting how it was now, believing if I just changed or worked hard enough, I could make it 'right' again. I'd do so much to try and please my partner that I forgot about myself, stopping doing the things *I* liked. After a few years of this behaviour, I forgot who I really was and lost all my joy. This led to feeling deeply depressed and thinking my only option was to end the relationship. I'd then grieve and feel devastated, believing I'd failed again, and there must be something deeply wrong with me. When I ended relationships, it wasn't because I fell out of love with my partners, but because the relationship was just too depressing, and I couldn't make it work no matter how much I tried to change: I dreaded the thought my partner would meet, and find happiness with, another woman. I believed if that happened, it would prove *I* wasn't good enough or that *she* had the 'right formula'.

I know now I was actually wishing they *wouldn't* find happiness. I've come to realise that my wishing unhappiness for them was simply so that *I* might not experience feeling like a failure ... and that was never going to work! The truth is, whatever I wish for someone else is *exactly* what I draw to myself; it's like how hating someone who's hurt you just poisons *you*, not them. This is why it's so important to genuinely wish others the best. But back then, I wasn't aware of my flawed thinking; because of my low sense of self-worth, I also wasn't able to control my negative thoughts and behaviours. Now I know the belief running me at the time was that I wasn't good enough, and it overrode my ability to want happiness for my partners in another relationship.

The final long-term relationship I was in ended very differently from the others. That time, I wasn't distraught for months after it ended because, somehow, I just knew we were done ... and that was okay!

I'd 'ended' the relationship many times before, but I clearly wasn't yet ready to admit it was never really going to work. After one particularly terrible argument, I felt incredibly traumatised. We'd had worse arguments than that one, but my reaction was different: My whole body shook inside and out for a couple of days afterwards, followed by a sense of numbness. I reflected on our time together and, from a place of utter desperation and yet also calmness, I saw how futile it was for us to stay together. For the first time, I realised we simply were *not* a match. We'd argued so many times because we disagreed about what love meant in a relationship. It was extremely frustrating for both of us to try and work through our incompatibilities.

In that moment, I stopped making myself *or* him wrong, which I'd certainly never been able to do before. In the past, I'd believed so much in 'right' and 'wrong' that I'd blame *one* of us for being the 'bad' one. But without this belief running me, all my judgments about him left, and I felt immense peace. I no longer felt the need to remember all the 'bad' things about him to justify letting him go.

When we said goodbye to each other, we hugged and I blessed him, wishing him nothing but happiness. I asked him to let go of trying to make the relationship work with me and move on with his life. I told him I wanted him to find true happiness with someone else, and I meant it with all my heart. I didn't say it because I thought I *should*. I just said it because it was true. It was freeing, and I knew *something* was different.

As soon as he left, alone in my villa, for the first time ever I grieved the relationship from a place of release, not regret or a sense of victimhood. I allowed myself to cry as deeply as possible, holding nothing back. As I allowed myself that grief, I let go of all the dreams I'd carried for so long about how we could make the relationship work. I cried until I was exhausted. I flopped on my bed with a feeling in my whole being of lightness and complete peace. It was like I'd released six years of struggle!

As I lay there, I suddenly felt the lightness in my body ripple over my heart and my tears of sadness transformed into hilarious laughter. I laughed so hard I felt ecstatic! I allowed myself to fully feel the laughter until I was once more totally exhausted. As I collapsed on the bed again, my body tingled with feelings of peace and serenity. The process felt complete: Not one ounce of sadness lingered, and my whole body felt totally relaxed. I went to bed that night feeling truly free. I sent lots of love and blessings to my ex-partner and drifted peacefully to sleep.

When I awoke the next morning, I felt an overwhelming desire for a deeper connection with God. I wanted to truly feel God's love for me and my love for God. I finally understood that, in order to have a truly healthy romantic relationship, I needed to first *only* desire the powerful Love of God. I needed to become the cup that overflowed with love, not the cup that was running on empty.

I saw that my low self-esteem was a sure indication my cup was indeed empty, and it would never be filled by someone outside of me (especially a man). I remembered the Booming Voice I'd heard that'd said to me, 'Be wanted by God and not a man.' I knew this didn't mean it was *wrong* to be in a relationship with a man, but that I first needed to accept God's unconditional love for me *just as I am*. Only then would I not feel the need to try and change myself to be accepted by another. With this newfound focus, my true spiritual journey began.

At the age of 56, I finally embarked on a journey back to wholeness, letting go of the illusion that any man could fulfil me. I came to clearly see that to place that responsibility on someone else was unfair – and it would never work, anyway! I've come to understand it was *never* meant to work that way; if it did, we'd never stop looking for happiness outside ourselves. We'd never return to the infinite Love within us, which is God's love.

It's said we're three-fold beings: of mind, body and spirit. If we don't seek to connect to the loving spirit within us but live instead only from our mind and body connections, we'll never truly feel fulfilled. We'll never know *how* to love unconditionally. When we truly *know* we're loved by that which gave us life (God), everything changes. We accept that Love is who we are, and that's why:

Love Will Set Us Free!

Chapter 15

Healing From Feeling Suicidal

Have you ever really stopped to notice how often you berate yourself? Have you ever noticed you probably say more cruel words about yourself than you would *ever* say about someone else? Self-doubt may arise now and again, but if you catch yourself repeatedly saying genuinely hurtful things to yourself in your mind, I urge you to stop, now, and know you *can* question them.

We need to realise we're *not* the unconscious, chattering voice in our head that constantly fills our mind with negative thoughts – especially critical ones. When we recognise this is happening and choose to question our negative thoughts to determine if they're really true, we're on our way to setting ourselves free from suffering. We are, in fact, the consciousness that comes from a loving voice within that speaks *only* of love and non-judgment, and that voice *is* within each of us. If you can become aware of your inner critic, you can question the negative beliefs you have about yourself, others, and the world.

This particular episode in my life is a perfect example of how damaging it can be to consistently think negative thoughts about ourselves.

When my children were around the ages of three, eight and ten, I left my partner to be with another man. At the time, I thought he was the love of my life, and we eventually married. It didn't take long for me to discover he had a serious problem with alcohol. Over a period of two years, I became obsessed with trying to get him to see he had a problem. I truly believed if he just stopped drinking, all my problems would disappear, and life would be wonderful.

The more I focused on his drinking, the worse he reacted to me. He insisted *I* was the problem. After a while, I started to believe there *was* something terribly wrong with me, because I couldn't make everything 'right'. I began to feel like a complete failure. I wanted to cry all the time, managing to keep it from my children by going into the bedroom or bathroom to do it quietly. Eventually, it affected me physically; I suffered from severe headaches almost every day. One day, the pain became so intense I couldn't get out of bed. This made me even more depressed, because now I couldn't even look after my children! I felt totally useless. I wanted to die and started to think more and more about taking my own life.

One day, as I sat on my bed, rocking and crying, my mind

repeatedly told me, 'The world will be better off without you. You're no good as a wife, you're no good as a daughter and you're no good as a mother.' I started to think seriously about how I could end my life. I contemplated all the different ways I could go through with it. I finally decided taking tablets would be the easiest option.

Suddenly, I heard a softer voice in my head say, 'Do you really believe your children would be better off without you?' Although this voice sounded like my own inner voice, it was no longer condemning me. Instead, it sounded tender, kind and loving.

Immediately, I felt how much I loved my sons and realized how devastated they'd be if I wasn't around. I even realised in that moment I was, indeed, a good mum, and no one could love them as much as I did.

This other, softer voice shook me out of my negative thinking. I awakened out of the lie I'd been hearing for years. That lie was the negative self-talk in my head that I'd believed was my friend. I was shocked! I realised I'd listened to that negative voice for so long I'd somehow allowed it to talk me into ending my life, convincing me I was totally worthless. This softer voice was different. It was loving and warm, wanting me to thrive and feel good about myself. I now refer to this loving voice as coming from my higher self, or God. Perhaps the condemning, negative self-talk is what the Bible refers to as the Devil or Satan, but I prefer to call it the ego.

～

I can't emphasise enough how important it is that we pause and question the condemning voice when we notice it criticizing us. Anything other than a voice that uplifts us is *not* the truth – it's ego. That voice is *not* who you are; the truth of who you are will come from the voice that's *always* loving and kind. But you'll only be able to hear the loving voice if you question the condemning one.

God is all loving and only has total, unconditional love for each one of us. By listening to the loving voice within, we'll be aligning with the certainty that:

Love is Truth and Love Will Set You Free!

Chapter 16

Healing Panic Attacks and Fear

When I was a teenager, I experienced panic attacks. At the time, I thought I was going crazy. I kept it mainly to myself because when I *did* speak about it, I wasn't understood, which left me feeling extremely depressed. I'm now 56 years old, and I hope and trust there's now more compassion and understanding for those who experience such attacks. If you've ever suffered from them, you may relate to this story. Not every panic attack happens for the same reason, but knowing how mine came to an end just might help you experience healing in the same way.

When I was 17 years old, I was in Florida with my father, staying with friends just after a weightlifting competition. One evening, they offered my father and I some weed to smoke. At that time, I didn't drink alcohol, and everyone else was getting drunk. My father had been drinking whisky; to my knowledge, this was the first time he'd ever smoked marijuana. After trying it himself, he suggested I take a drag, but I refused. He became very angry, saying, 'For God's sake, let your hair down for once and try some.' So, I did.

The result was me laughing hysterically and feeling unbelievably free. I didn't experience any negative after effects, unlike with alcohol, which can result in a hangover the next day. I also didn't feel the need or desire to do it again until a year later, when I found myself staying with the same family, this time without my father present.

One evening, we went out to a bar with live music. Little did I know their intention was also to buy and smoke marijuana again. They started smoking it in the car on the way and offered me some. I remembered how great it'd been before and that I hadn't suffered any negative side effects. So, I decided to inhale a huge drag and hold it in as long as I could. After about three drags, we arrived at the bar.

As we walked in, I started feeling a little strange. By the time I sat down on the bar stool, I was experiencing a horrible, strange sensation in my left ear. This weird feeling started to consume me, and I felt dread flooding my entire body. My heart started to race and pound so hard I thought it was going to explode out of my chest. I was terrified! The fear was so intense, I ran out of the bar, crying. My friends came running after me. The feeling was so unbearable, I wanted to run out in front of a car to get away from the intense feeling of terror consuming my body and mind. (I've since discovered smoking marijuana can sometimes bring on paranoia and fear, which obviously happened to me that night).

Luckily, my friends caught me and put me in the back of

the car, holding me down to stop me from running into traffic. I was lying face down, screaming. I heard them patiently telling me to take some deep breaths, reassuring me it would soon pass if I just tried to relax. It took about 30 minutes for the fear to finally leave. I was utterly exhausted.

When they were sure I was calm enough, my friends stopped holding me down, and we drove home. The next day, when I thought about the incident, my heart started to race again and I experienced another panic attack, exactly as I had the night before. Fear once again consumed my entire body. It was like when I felt depressed, but a hundred times worse. All I remember was sitting on the end of my bed thinking I was going to feel like this for the rest of my life, which of course intensified the feeling of fear. Eventually, it subsided without me wanting to end my life like I had the night before. But the experience was still terrifying.

Unfortunately, these attacks continued for nine months, occurring at least once a day. I only had to think about the fear, and it would return. I didn't seem able to stop thinking about it; I was living in a constant state of fear of the next panic attack happening.

One day, after months of suffering from the attacks and dreading another one coming, I wondered if I could come to some sort of acceptance around them. I pondered if it might be possible to not live in so much fear of the next one occurring, knowing I may have them for the rest of my life. That's when I heard a question come into my mind: 'Have you not noticed that they *always* pass?' *Hmm*, I thought, *what if, when the next time one happens, I just don't fight against it?*

And that's exactly what I did: When the next panic attack

arose a few hours later, I chose to lie down and accept it was happening, telling myself it would pass. I was able to calm myself down by breathing deeply and slowly, which helped relax my body and mind. The attack passed very quickly since I was no longer fighting it. That was the last panic attack I ever had.

I discovered through this direct experience that acceptance dissolves fear. Fighting against something I don't want will actually make it worse! Once I no longer dreaded the panic attacks recurring, they disappeared. The key to the miracle came by knowing all I had to do was reassure myself it would pass, relax and be *with* the fear when it arose, rather than denying or giving in to it. It was fear of fear itself that I finally overcame! By bringing love and acceptance to the situation, I allowed the miracle to take place. Love really does equal miracles!

This was the first time the voice I now call my higher Self spoke to me, asking me the very question I needed to hear to bring me back to Truth. I discovered that in the presence of Love, fear cannot exist, once again showing me that:

Love is Truth and Love Will Set You Free!

Chapter 17

Angels to the Rescue

About 20 years ago, on a gorgeous, sunny day in England, my then-partner and I went out on a bike ride along the canal. We'd been out many times before, usually with the children. On this occasion, I was cycling in front of him. I turned off the path from the canal near to the road where we were going to have lunch at a nearby pub. My partner was only about 20 or 30 metres behind me. When I stopped at the road, I looked back, but he was nowhere to be seen. I waited and waited, but he didn't arrive. A horrifying thought suddenly struck me: *I hope he hasn't fallen in the canal!* This was particularly scary because I knew he couldn't swim.

I cycled back as quickly as I could. As I turned onto the path, there he was, right in the middle of the canal! There was no bike to be seen; it had already sunk under the deep water where he'd fallen in. For someone who couldn't swim, he managed to keep his head above water quite well, but he was fighting an extremely strong current and so wasn't actually getting anywhere. I could see he was tiring very quickly. I knew I couldn't jump in to try to save him because I wasn't strong enough to hold him up and swim through the current. I remember thinking, *Oh my God, I'm going to have to watch him drown and there's nothing I can do about it!* Significant memories of our life together flashed through my mind.

I suddenly noticed two people approaching me–a young man and woman who appeared to be in their late twenties. They said nothing. Without any hesitation, the man started to take off his jacket. I shouted out, 'He can't swim'! I thought the man was about to jump into the canal to save my partner, but instead he got as close to the edge of the bank as possible and then asked me to hold on to his hand. He took hold of the end of one of his jacket sleeves and threw the jacket out to my partner to grab onto the other sleeve. It's amazing how long a jacket can extend out when you don't have a pole or large branch at hand to reach someone! My partner managed to grab the jacket sleeve almost immediately, and the man pulled him quickly and safely back to the bank.

I said to my partner, 'Oh my God, you nearly drowned'! He replied, 'I was doing okay'. In my anxiousness and relief, I cried out, 'Do you realise you were getting nowhere because of the current? This man just saved your life'! I could see it suddenly strike my partner what this person had actually done for him. We both turned around to thank the man, but both he and the woman had disappeared. My partner told me to try and find them. He wanted to buy the man a drink and say thank you. I ran up the path to see if they had turned off, but they were nowhere to be seen. I could see a long way in both directions up the path and there was no sight of them. I even ran into the nearby pub, but I couldn't find them anywhere. They just seemed to vanish.

After the rescue, I started reading all about angels appearing and saving people's lives. I'd always believed in angels but didn't realise they could appear in human form until this experience.

To this day, I think if the young man and woman who appeared that day had been normal human beings, surely, they would have hung around long enough to ask us both if we were okay.

While we'll obviously never really know or be able to prove the young man and woman were angels, I *have* since heard and read many stories where people have been saved from death by someone who suddenly appears and then vanishes without a trace after the rescue. This brings me so much comfort, knowing we're not alone, and there are spiritual beings looking after us if it isn't yet time to leave our physical bodies.

Angels are described as having a very loving presence, and Love was definitely there that day to literally set my partner free from drowning! For:

Love is Trust, and Love Will Set You Free!

Chapter 18

The Miracle of Overcoming Physical Pain

Physical pain can be one of the hardest things to bear. Intense pain suffered continuously for long periods of time can certainly bring up all sorts of debilitating beliefs about ourselves and disbelief in a loving God. For so many years, the pain I experienced led me to beat myself up. I believed I was somehow being punished. I had a mantra in my head that insisted I must be doing something wrong to deserve such continuous pain.

At the age of seven, I started to get headaches. Over time, they became more and more painful. When I was about 11, the pain was so bad that I tried to knock myself out by hitting my head against my bedroom wall. Obviously, it didn't work – it just made the headache worse. Many times, I longed for someone to put me to sleep with an injection so I would never have to wake up and face the pain again. It was so intense at times, it would make my whole body shake and convulse, and I always had to take painkillers to get rid of these types of headaches. Other times, I'd get a headache that was more bearable across my eyes and forehead, but this type made me feel sick. Painkillers didn't work on them, and sometimes the headaches would last for days. I noticed they were particularly bad when I was under stress or depressed. The headaches continued throughout my life.

In my mid-forties, I was holding a study group meeting at my house for the book *A Course in Miracles*, which contains teachings from Jesus about how to transform your life by choosing Love over fear. A small group gathered at my house every week where we would do our best to understand the powerful messages in the text. We'd been gathering for a few years at this point. On one particular evening, one of the members made a comment that brought us all to total silence. They said something like, 'If someone as loving as Jesus got put to death, I'm not sure following His teachings is very safe.'

When everyone left that night, we were all more quiet than usual. I know I was. I'd had the idea that if I could become as loving and kind as Jesus, then my life would get better. Now I was questioning that assumption. I went into the kitchen and stood by my window, looking out at the garden, contemplating what had been discussed. Then I heard very clearly in my head, 'You don't understand. I didn't suffer on the cross because I did not make it *wrong*, unlike you with your headaches.'

As I heard these words, my first thought was, *Wherever*

this information is coming from, Jesus or not, how do they know me so well? For it was true that every time I got a headache, I'd always make them wrong or think *I'd* done something wrong to deserve them. I'd conclude that I hadn't eaten right, that God didn't love me enough or maybe even that I was being punished, but, for sure, I definitely made them *wrong*. So, wherever these words were coming from, they were the perfect words for me to hear.

Then the voice very quickly said, 'Can you find one reason to be *grateful* for your headaches?' Immediately, without any thinking whatsoever, I knew the answer. If it wasn't for the headaches, I'd never have sought healing for them, which opened my mind up in so many different ways. I'd read about angels, positive thinking, healing through prayer and, especially, the healing gift of Love. I felt so much gratitude in that moment. It filled my heart, and I became so truly grateful for the headaches, recognizing how different my life would have been without them. I'd gained so much wisdom and become so much more peaceful than I was before.

In the past, people had said to me, 'You've got to love the pain of the headaches in order for them to go away.' This felt very dismissive of my experience, and I'd feel so angry inside because there was no way I could love the pain itself. But feeling immense gratitude for what they'd brought me was very different from trying to love the actual pain. I also discovered that by bringing Love through gratitude to the situation, rather than condemning myself or God for why it was happening, was a vital key to transformation. The gratitude helped me accept the pain rather than tighten and fight against it, which always caused the pain to intensify. I'd been fighting the pain since my very first headache at the age of seven. I didn't know a way to find acceptance for the headaches until I heard this communication from Jesus.

Immediately after hearing that message to find gratitude for the headaches, suddenly in a flash I had the most terrible headache! This wasn't normal for me. Usually, I'd feel a headache coming on and have some warning, but not this time. I couldn't forget the message I'd just heard, so I went straight to my bed to lie down. I took some deep breaths and tried to calm myself by not tightening or contracting my body or making the headaches *wrong*. Instead, I thanked the headaches for all they'd brought me. I even put a big smile on my face, despite the fact I was in a great deal of pain. I did this for about five minutes. Suddenly, the pain turned to ecstasy! My body felt so light, I thought I was going to lift off the bed and float to the ceiling. The next thing I knew, it was morning. I'd fallen asleep and woken up without a trace of a headache! My first thought as I awoke was, *Oh my God, I really did hear Jesus speak to me! I did what he suggested, and a miracle happened!*

We truly can transmute pain when we fully surrender to the moment, knowing and trusting that it will pass. Feeling gratitude (once we can see things from a different perspective) is extremely powerful. When we can truly relax and allow what's happening from a place of acceptance, love and gratitude for what's unfolding, we allow miracles to occur.

Since the day I heard that question from Jesus about finding gratitude for the pain of the headaches, I've only experienced two really painful ones, but now I know what to do: I breathe deeply and relax into the pain, *not* resisting it, and remember to thank the headaches for all the gifts that have come from them. I do still get the odd mild headache from time to time, but I never go into fear around them or make myself wrong. I'm convinced that's the reason they're not as painful as they were before. After all, the *opposite* of Love is fear and resistance.

Once again, my experience has shown me that Love *can* heal all things, proving that:

Love Truly is Truth, And Love Will Set You Free!

Chapter 19

Healing with Noisy Neighbours, Part One

Noise can be one of the most irritating things in life if we don't find a way to be at peace with it. I found myself having to deal with this situation over and over again until I was able to see – or in this case, hear – differently. It's very funny that, as humans, we've been conditioned to accept some noises as beautiful and others as not. Birds singing in the morning can be very loud, but most of us seem to take great delight in hearing the birds sing, no matter how loud they are.

I lived for a while in Bali, Indonesia, where the wildlife sounds are very loud and continue throughout the whole day. The constant sound of crickets and cockerels going on and off constantly didn't bother me at all. But one day while staying in my little villa, I heard really loud dance music and people talking and laughing very loudly. It was so loud that even if I put my headphones on, I could still hear the thumping of the bass vibrating. I discovered that someone new had moved into the villa behind me, which was only about six feet away. The noise was very disturbing, not like the peace I was used to.

I tried to accept the situation by telling myself it probably wouldn't last long, but it went on for hours. My first thought was how inconsiderate they were to move into a villa that was so close to another villa, knowing they were going to play such loud music. This happened a couple more times during the week. Finally, when it was going on late at night and I couldn't sleep, I went round and knocked on the door. They couldn't hear my knocking over the music, so I called out as politely as possible, 'Could you please turn the music down a bit? I can't sleep!' Thankfully, they turned it down, and I thought it might not happen again now they were aware it was disturbing someone.

A few days later, the music started up again during the day, and it seemed to be even louder than before. I could see into the room of the villa when the curtains were open, and I could see and hear very clearly that a man was giving dance lessons. I realised I'd seen this man before at a festival; he was, indeed, a very good dancer. I found myself once again judging him. I was thinking he was very rude; he may be a good dancer, but he clearly wasn't a very nice person!

At the time, I was becoming more and more aware when my mind would automatically start judging. I'd been praying frequently to God to help me judge less and love more. So, as I caught myself having these judgemental thoughts, I decided to sit down and think before rushing over to complain. I thought to myself, *I know what I'll do. I'll go around to his villa and politely suggest that he get some Bluetooth*

earphones so they can play loud music without disturbing anyone.
But I wanted to be sure this thought wasn't coming from my
ego; something felt a bit off. This time, I remembered to
breathe deeply and slowly for a time and ask for guidance
from a higher source of Love, something I've learned to do
that takes me out of my egoic thinking mind and allows me
to access how Love would respond. Some would call this
connecting to God, Holy Spirit, a Higher Power, or Source.

The guidance came very quickly. I heard a gentle voice
say, 'Get to know him by going around and introducing
yourself *first* as his neighbour.' I was to tell him that I'd seen
him at a festival and thought he was a *very* good dancer. I
also heard that, instead of offering my advice to him about
Bluetooth, I was to ask for *his* advice on how we could make
this situation work for *both* of us. The thought of speaking
with him in this way brought up some fear, but not as much
as my first idea, which was to give him *my* advice. (How many
people respond well to us giving them our advice when it
isn't asked for?) I decided to *not* go to his villa when he was
playing loud music but wait until the time felt right. I've
learned to be patient, because the ego *always* wants to rush
in and attempt to fix things straightaway. So, I asked for
guidance to be shown the perfect time.

Later that day, I went to get some groceries. On the way
back, I came face-to-face with my neighbour on the path that
led back to my villa; as I turned a corner, my eyes met his. In
that moment, all I could see was my son looking back at me. I
immediately heard, 'If he *was* your son, how would you feel
if he was living next door to you, giving dance lessons?' At
that moment, I realised I'd be delighted if *any* of my sons

were living such a wonderful life, using their gifts and living their dreams. I'd be so much more patient, accommodating and joyful. Tears filled my eyes as this revelation hit me.

The next day, I could see my neighbour in his villa, and everything was very quiet. It felt like a good time to go see him. I was a little nervous and noticed my heart starting to beat faster at the thought of doing so. Once again, I found myself needing to be patient, so I sat down and took some deep breaths until I felt calmer. I felt a warm energy come over me as I remembered the revelation from the previous day, and I began to relax again. I remembered, as I went round to see him, to go with the intention of just getting to know him.

I knocked on the door, and as he answered, I smiled. He had a very welcoming look on his face, which was a relief to me. I asked if he had a few spare minutes. He said yes and invited me to have a seat. I started the conversation by telling him that I'd seen him dance once or twice at a couple of events and thought he was a very good dancer. I expressed that I really didn't want to spoil his fun or be a killjoy, but wanted him to know that, because we live so close, his music was a bit too loud. I also told him I went to bed quite early and wondered if he had any suggestions as to how we could resolve the noise problem? He acted very kindly and with great understanding. He said he didn't want to disturb me, and offered his number so I could call him anytime if the music was too loud. He also suggested that he could let me know a day or two in advance if he was going to host a dance class, so I could plan to go out if I wanted to.

The communication felt really good. I knew it went so

amazingly well *because* I'd taken the time to breathe and ask for guidance first. I also feel that my Higher Self guided me to see him as my son, which helped me become open to Love's way and not my ego's way. Thank goodness I didn't act on my first thought, which was to go around and give him some of my advice!

Only one week went by before I saw him again on the same path. He told me he'd found a much more suitable villa to do his work in that had no neighbours close by, and he was moving out the next day. I wished him all the best, and I meant it with all my heart.

When we ask for guidance – especially when we're triggered by something – we give God's loving support a chance to work. From my experience, it *always* brings these delightful miracles. When we breathe and connect to the Truth, love shows us the answer. And that's why:

Love is Truth and Love Will Set Us Free!

Chapter 20

Healing with Noisy Neighbours, Part Two

Two weeks after the dancing man moved out, I was getting ready for bed when I heard a really high-pitched wailing sound coming from a different villa on the other side of mine. The sound was haunting and *very* unpleasant. It was so loud that even when I put in my ear plugs, I could still hear the noise. It remained unbelievably loud for over 20 minutes. I became so triggered that I forgot to breathe, pause, and ask for guidance. I couldn't stand it, so I went outside and said very politely, 'Could you please turn the sound down? I can't sleep!' As with my previous neighbour, this one couldn't hear me over the sound. So, I repeated myself, but this time I had to shout really loudly. Eventually, they turned it down.

A few days later, the strange sound started up again at the same time. Once more, I went outside and asked the neighbour to please turn it down. I didn't like having to shout over the garden fence because it felt so impersonal. I decided the next day, I'd go and knock on my neighbour's door to introduce myself, as I had done with the dancing man. I'd go with the intention of getting to know them and ask what their advice would be so we could live next door to each other in harmony. This time, I remembered to sit down and take some deep breaths before going around to speak with them. As I approached the villa, I saw through the glass door a young woman sitting on her couch. When she noticed me coming, she came to the door, and I introduced myself as her next-door neighbour.

First, I apologised for having shouted so loudly over the fence the previous day, saying I felt I *had* to shout to be heard. I explained that I didn't like having to shout so loudly, and wondered if there was any chance she could *not* play the sounds so late and so loud at night? She was polite but also quite agitated. At first, I thought I'd upset her, and she was just trying not to show it, but she explained she was also dealing with very loud construction noise on the other side of *her* villa. She also said that the sounds I heard from her were vocal expressions of sound healing she was giving to people online. The participants lived on the other side of the world, so she couldn't offer it any other time.

She told me she'd been upset that I'd disturbed her session by shouting so loudly, as she was trying to help people in Covid lockdown situations. I listened, agreeing that what she was doing was indeed very kind. I also explained again that I didn't like having to shout over the wall at her but, at the time, didn't know what else to do. I then asked her if she had a solution to our dilemma. She explained that because of the construction noise, she felt it was time to move to a more suitable place to do her sound healing anyway. I asked if she was willing to swap telephone numbers so she could let me know in advance when she'd be doing her next session. She appreciated my understanding and agreed to this suggestion.

I felt led to ask her if she would like to go for coffee or juice sometime at our local cafe, as I'd love to know more about her sound healing. Her face lit up at the idea, and we met the following day. We had a wonderful talk about our own healing journeys and became much closer. A couple of days later, she told me she'd found another place to live where there was no construction, and that it was a much more suitable place for her sound healing. She moved out the following week. We stayed on good terms.

This may not seem like a huge miracle, but it's yet another example of how genuine, loving communication can bring about beautiful resolutions. In contrast, a typical ego reaction is to quickly make an enemy of someone we feel is 'disturbing' our peace.

I've learnt over the years how precious it is to get to know someone (and their situation) rather than allowing judgement to rule my actions. I've found time and again how healing it is when we become genuinely interested in another person's circumstances. We may not always be able to stop the mind's first reaction of judgement when we're initially disturbed. But we can learn to *not* act upon our first egoic thoughts and, instead, choose love and understanding.

This takes a commitment to awareness and vigilance over time to remember to pause and ask for love's guidance.

Love *always* reveals the Truth. Our thinking mind usually doesn't, *especially* when we're triggered. But:

Love is Truth and Love Will Set You Free!

Chapter 21

Healing With Noisy Neighbours, Part Three

I wasn't done yet with noisy neighbours. The next new neighbour presented me with another opportunity to receive even more healing around acceptance of noise. It felt like God *really* wanted me to overcome this issue!

For the third time in one month, another person moved into the neighbouring villa. The previous tenant, who I'd made friends with, told me the new person moving in was a lovely man who offered healing massage treatments, so there should be no problems with loud noises this time. One thing she did say (in humour) was that I might hear the odd yell or scream if he hit a sore point when massaging someone. I was extremely relieved, thinking I'd learnt all I needed to about accepting loud noises, and all would be well.

Two days went by, and all was peaceful. On the second

evening, around seven o'clock, I started hearing screaming sounds, like someone was being attacked. This was followed by crying. At first, I thought it was a couple having a fight, but then I heard really hard slapping sounds followed by screaming and crying. It sounded so violent, it made me feel physically sick. It continued, the slapping getting harder. The woman's screaming caused a shuddering throughout my body. I couldn't believe this was happening again! It wasn't just a slightly irritating sound but yet another extreme occurrence of something I considered unbearable.

The noise was so intense, I completely forgot to sit and breathe first before taking any action. I determined the sounds weren't two people having a fight, but the type of massage my new neighbour was performing on someone. I felt angry and a sense of complete disbelief that someone could be doing this so close to where someone else was living! My reactive mind told me that this person *must* be a masochist pretending to be a healer, and people were falling for it! Of course, I had no proof of this, and the thought made me feel even worse about the situation.

I wasn't aware enough at the time to catch my mind making up all these judgements, so I found myself calling over the fence yet again, this time speaking in a very demanding way. I shouted, 'Will you please stop doing whatever it is you're doing because the noise is very disturbing!' Immediately, the noises stopped, and two people came out of the villa to speak with me. One was a man, and the other was a woman wearing a robe. She told me she was sorry, but he didn't speak much English and she only spoke a little. She continued, saying she was sorry for the noise, but that he was giving her a healing session.

My body was still shaking from hearing the screams and slapping sounds, so I replied, 'I don't care *what* you're doing, please stop. It sounds so violent!' I told them I could hear every slap and scream, and this was *not* the place to be doing it, right next to where someone else is living. I couldn't see either of them very well, as we were talking through a fence and some bushes that separated our villas. She said they were very sorry if they'd upset me. I was so relieved at their response, it almost brought me to tears. I thanked them for understanding and went back into my villa. The noise stopped. I was hopeful it really wouldn't happen again.

I started to wonder why I was still attracting these unbelievable situations with neighbours and noise. I thought I had learnt much about loving communication and felt a little disappointed in myself that I'd reacted in fear instead of asking for guidance first. Of course, feeling disappointed with oneself is coming from ego, not Love, and luckily, I was able to catch what I was doing. Even though what I said in frustration stopped the noisy session, my heart still wanted to have a more understanding connection with this man and to see things more clearly from a loving perspective. I wanted to find out more about his healing modality and see if I could let go of my judgemental thoughts around it.

This time, there was an added problem since he didn't speak English. I prayed and asked for guidance as to how I could make some connection with this new neighbour. I reminded myself how healing it had been before, getting to know someone instead of choosing to believe the thoughts my mind loved to make up about them. I realised that if I could find someone who could interpret for me, maybe I could make a connection with my neighbour. I'd learned he was Russian, so I prayed I would find an interpreter quickly so we could resolve the issue as soon as possible.

The following day, I heard the side gate to my villa open and someone call out 'hello'. Two men were standing at the door. I recognised one of them as my neighbour, and the other introduced himself as a friend who had come to interpret for him. My prayer had been answered! I felt a little anxious, as they were rather large men with tattoos, and I had no idea whether they were coming in peace or whether they would try to be intimidating. But the first thing my neighbour said (in Russian), with his hand on his heart, was that he was truly sorry about what happened the night before. His friend interpreted his words into English. I could see from my neighbour's body language that he *had* come in peace. I was delighted. My desire to have some personal communication with this man had been resolved without me even trying!

I believe just by having the willingness to desire the most loving outcome for all concerned is all it takes for our loving Source / God to make it happen. This was yet another little miracle for me to witness. The interpreter went on to say that this particular client had come to see my neighbour many times, and it was *not* how a typical session would be. My neighbour assured me it wouldn't happen again, and he was also going to change the room in which he did his sessions to one that was further away from my villa. Without me even asking, he offered his number and asked me to text or call him if at *any* time he was disturbing me. This felt wonderful. I thanked God for this amazing outcome. It again reaffirmed the power of choosing Love over fear.

A few days went by. I could hear my neighbour was having a small gathering of friends at his villa. It was a little noisy but nothing very disturbing. I heard someone calling out my name from over the garden fence, and in his broken English, my neighbour asked me to come around and join the party. I'd been about to go to bed early but decided to accept his invitation. When someone offers me a gift in *any* form, I find reasons to say 'Yes' rather than 'No'. I won't be a people-pleaser or doormat for anyone and have no problem saying no to something I really don't want to do, but I *will* inquire within before saying no to someone's request or offer.

When I arrived at my neighbour's, I discovered a few of his friends there spoke English. He told me (through their interpreting) he'd heard me singing in the mornings in a different language, and he liked it so much that he'd recorded it on his phone. He was referring to the Lord's prayer, which I sing in Aramaic (the language Jesus spoke). I often start my day singing this prayer. The tone in which I sing it, along with the vibration of the language itself, always brings me into a state of great peace. I've sung this powerful prayer in various places around the world, and most people who've heard it were moved by the powerful vibration that comes through. I felt it must have also touched my neighbour in some way for him to have wanted to record it.

I thanked him for sharing this with me, and one of his friends asked if I would sing it for them. I agreed and invited them to close their eyes and feel the vibration of the prayer. When the prayer song ended, you could hear a pin drop. No one spoke for quite a while. The atmosphere in the room completely shifted to one of peace. It was a very beautiful moment, and they expressed their appreciation deeply. I thanked everyone there for allowing me to share the prayer with them. I left the party feeling so much gratitude for how everything had unfolded.

My neighbour and I continued to live next to each other very peacefully, and I never heard another scream or slap from his sessions. He only stayed another month. I assumed he'd found a more suitable place to live. Once again, I experienced that when I look for the loving answer, it's shown to me, and all *can* be resolved peacefully. After all:

Love is *Definitely* the Answer and Love Will Set Us *All* Free!

If you'd like to hear me singing The Lord's Prayer *in Aramaic, please visit the following link:* **https://youtu.be/ aCAS31M7mlA**

Chapter 22

Healing With Noisy Neighbours, Part Four

Three weeks later, another new neighbour moved in, right behind my own villa. It was a young man, and almost straightaway he started playing very loud, heavy rap music. This music was even louder than the dance music from the previous neighbour. The bass was very strong, and the thumping sound vibrated through my entire villa. Once again, even using earplugs or listening to my own music with earphones didn't drown out the sound.

I couldn't believe it! I really thought I'd learnt all I needed to come to peace with noisy neighbours, and yet here I was, experiencing yet again a sound that was very hard to live with. By this time, I was feeling quite worn down by it all and wondered what I still needed to see differently. I thought perhaps this was life showing me that it was time to move somewhere else, but I loved my little villa and had made it my home. This time, I didn't go over to speak with the young man right away, but instead decided to wait and see if the loud music would stop.

The music continued the whole day. Around 8pm, I decided to go knock on my new neighbour's door to politely ask him to turn the music down since I was about to go to bed. Once again, when I knocked on the door and called out 'hello', he couldn't hear me over the sound of the music. I knocked a bit louder, and eventually he came to the door. I was slightly shocked at his appearance; half of his face was tattooed, and he was wearing some scary yellowish contact lenses. He didn't look very pleased, but he agreed to turn the music down. The volume lowered slightly, but it was enough for me to get to sleep with my earplugs in, so I was very grateful.

The next day, the music started up again in the morning. This time, it was louder, with an even stronger bass sound. I felt sad and also a bit angry at my neighbour's defiance. I wanted to cry, but I thought I could try one more time to see if he'd be willing to turn the music down a little. I didn't sit and ask for guidance – I was really allowing my ego to get the better of me! Feeling agitated, I went over and knocked on his door. Again, there was no answer. I shouted out 'hello' really loudly just to be heard and, eventually, he appeared at the upstairs balcony. He said, 'You're brave, coming around here again'. I replied, 'I just wondered if you could turn it down a little bit? It's so loud and our villas are very close to each other.' Despite my polite request he replied, 'Don't come 'round here again! I am not turning it down.' He was so adamant in his response, I knew there was nothing I could say or do to make him change his mind. Surprisingly, I was very calm, accepting there would be no sense in trying again.

As I walked back to my villa, I thought my only option might be to move somewhere else. For four years, I'd lived there in peace with no issues, and it'd only been over the last two months that I'd encountered all these problems with neighbours.

The following day, I looked at some other villas. Nothing I looked at was anywhere nearly as wonderful as where I was staying. I realised I loved where I was living and thought there must be another way. I remembered my most important compass in my life was to follow what I loved and not run away from my fears. I decided to use a worksheet created by Byron Katie called *Love Your Neighbour,* which helps us question our beliefs. In this case, I needed to get to the bottom of why this noise was causing me so much distress.

At first, it all seemed hopeless. My problem, after all, was the neighbour playing very loud music. If I turned the situation around to its opposite meaning, as Katie suggests, and said the neighbour *wasn't* playing loud music, it would definitely be untrue. So instead, I questioned my beliefs about the music itself. I discovered I had a belief that the loud rap music was going to harm me because it was harsh and had a low vibration. When I really thought about it, I realised I had no true evidence for this. The other belief was that if I put earplugs in during the day to drown out the noise, they'd somehow damage my hearing. Once again, I had no real evidence of this being true and realised my mind was simply making up all these beliefs.

I saw it was the actual beliefs hurting me far more than the music being played. In fact, it was even possible that if I put earplugs in during the day to block out the loud music, maybe I would find my villa even more peaceful than I had before. As for the music itself, I realised that just because the music he was playing was not of my liking, it didn't mean it was going to harm me. I started to laugh out loud at the ridiculousness of my thoughts. I felt myself feeling lighter and lighter as this new perspective dropped in and my fear started to diminish.

Other beliefs I discovered by inquiring into my thoughts were that this man was mean, inconsiderate, unkind and selfish. When I thought of him in this way, I felt angry and *extremely* self-righteous. Inquiry helped me see the errors of my thinking, so instead of believing these negative thoughts about him, I replaced them with new ones. What if he just really enjoyed playing this type of music all day long, and *I* was the one being selfish, mean, and inconsiderate? I saw that I believed I needed *him* to be different so that *I* could be happy. Once again, when I saw things differently from a less selfish perspective, I started to feel much more at peace. In that moment, I chose to accept that I couldn't always have my own way, and if I let go of trying to control the situation, all *would* eventually be okay.

The key to all of this is that when you find peace (through honest self-inquiry instead of using the 'logical' mind – which in my case told me to just move), the problems resolve themselves. Some would call this letting go and letting God in or surrendering what we can't control. The only thing I could control at that time (other than moving) was my own thoughts about the situation.

I felt grateful for what I'd discovered and thanked God I finally did the self-inquiry and got honest with myself! I felt a new sense of freedom and lightness at seeing the funny side of it all. I put my earplugs in during the day while the music played and looked out from my villa onto the beautiful rice fields. I felt an overwhelming sense of peace and contentment because I'd found the solution. I also noticed that, even without the earplugs, the music wasn't annoying me as much because I was no longer resisting and judging it. I felt so happy. My heart was so filled with joy, I could hardly believe it!

A few hours later, I decided to go for a walk to the local shops. I was still feeling so light and blissful, and I was beaming from ear to ear saying hello to everyone I met along the path. On the way, I could see my neighbour walking towards me. He was easily recognisable because of the tattoos on his face. As he got closer, all I could feel was appreciation for him. I looked right into his eyes and, with love in my heart, I gave him a big smile. I said 'hello' as I passed him, and he replied 'hello' back to me. It felt amazing!

Suddenly, in a flash before my eyes, I saw my neighbour as if he was my younger son. The love I have for my three sons is a love that's hard to express or put into words. All I wish for them is to be happy and content. In that moment, I felt so much more love for this young man. It truly felt like I was being helped by something far greater than myself. This vision of my younger son came to me seemingly from nowhere; it didn't feel like it came from my own thinking mind. A higher Source / God had given me an extra gift to help me warm to my neighbour even more by seeing him as one of my sons.

When I returned home, the music was still playing loudly, and yet all I could feel was immense love and appreciation for my new young neighbour. Once again, by seeing this young man as if he were one of my sons, just like I'd done with one of my previous noisy neighbours, it changed everything.

The music continued every day in the same way, and it never bothered me at all. For me, this was a miracle! Sometimes the music played, and I didn't even hear it. This truly showed me that when we awaken to Truth, we discover it isn't the situations in our lives that cause us suffering, but our thoughts *about* them that cause us pain. If we take the time to question our thoughts and give Love a chance, we give ourselves the opportunity to see things differently and return to peace.

I've found that when our desire for a loving outcome is genuinely sought, and our focus isn't only on ourselves, it allows amazing things to unfold. I continue to practice being aware of my mind's tendency to think the worst of someone when things aren't going 'my' way. It takes constant vigilance, and a deep desire, to be an expression of Love by not acting on the automatic reaction of my ego mind.

All these miracle stories came about because I chose Love over fear and judgement. It's through the seeking of Love that God can show us another way. When we sincerely seek for Truth, the Loving way is shown to us, and that's why:

Truth is Love, and It's *Always* LOVE That Sets Us Free!

Chapter 23

The Miracle of Shaving Off My Hair!

You may relate to this story if you've ever had an attachment to your appearance. For me, I decided this attachment had run my life for too long. This is my miracle story of how I managed to let go of much of that attachment.

When I started competitive diving at a young age, I was in chlorinated swimming pool water almost every day. It didn't take long for my strawberry blond hair to become very shiny due to the chlorine. I'd get stopped by strangers in the street asking what shampoo I used because my hair looked like shiny gold (as one woman remarked). I think this was the beginning of my obsession with my hair. I received so many compliments about my shiny hair wherever I went, I'd come to believe it was my *hair* that made me stand out and get noticed. There was a part of me that thought no one would ever see or love me if my hair was dull. I remember spending a great deal of time brushing my hair in front of the mirror so I could make it look just right. My family teased me about it, but I was too attached to my looks to stop (despite their mocking).

When I stopped competitive diving around the age of 14, my hair started darkening. I didn't like it at all. It didn't take me long to start dying my hair blond; the lighter the colour my hair was, the better I felt. I thought that if my hair was dull, then *I* was dull.

This belief continued throughout my life. I gradually became aware that if my hair *looked* good, I *felt* good ... and only then could I go out into the day feeling great. In contrast, when I had a 'bad' hair day, I'd feel extremely low and spend most of the day checking myself in the mirror to see if I could improve the way it looked. This was exhausting (and extremely obsessive).

When I was 35, I started going to Al-Anon, a Twelve Step Program for people affected by someone else's drinking. It was life transforming for me, enabling me to alter my perceptions, improve my sense of self-worth and take responsibility for my own actions and decisions (especially the beliefs that took away my peace). It also connected me to my spiritual self, a part I'd been disconnected from for so long. For the first time, life started making sense to me, especially as I became aware of my unhealthy thinking patterns.

After about ten years in Al-Anon, I met a woman at a Way of Mastery workshop in Bali who'd shaved her head to let go of her attachment to what she looked like. She said so many women think they wouldn't be loved if they didn't look a certain way, which immediately rang true for me. In that moment, I remembered how I was absolutely convinced that if I didn't look a certain way (meaning, have shiny, golden hair), no one would even *see* me, let alone love me. But despite the fact I so strongly related to what this woman was saying, I couldn't let go of the belief that no one would even give me a second look without my golden blond hair. I desperately wanted to shave my own hair off right then and there, but I just couldn't go through with it.

Over the next four years, this thought of shaving my head would come to me sporadically, especially when I was feeling unworthy about my appearance. I desperately wanted to be free of my obsession with my looks. I started to think about it more and more. I so wanted to be able to feel good about myself and my life no matter *how* I looked. Finally, I woke up one morning and knew that I was ready. I was co-facilitating a spiritual workshop in Ireland at the time, and it was the final day. What happened next was quite unbelievable.

The moment I decided I was definitely going through with shaving my head, my mind screamed out in resistance, saying, 'If you do this, you'll look so ugly you'll fall on the floor overwhelmed with grief. You'll become so depressed you'll end up in a mental home!' I remember, for just a moment, believing these thoughts ... and then suddenly, I heard something completely different in my mind. This new thought said, 'Wait a minute. That's just a choice. You could choose joy no matter what you look like!' I now know this voice to be my higher Self, or God's voice, that speaks only Truth and Love.

After hearing these words, I suddenly felt a tremendous excitement ripple through my body; all the fear around shaving my hair off left me immediately. I was ready, and I was going to do it *today*!

As the retreat was about to end, I announced what had happened to me that morning. I asked if anyone would be willing to come outside and help me shave all my hair off in the energy of Joy! Everyone agreed. It was a wonderfully hilarious experience! We only had one electric beard shaver, so each person took a turn shaving off some portion of my hair. Almost all of us wore clown noses throughout the whole thing, and we laughed continuously. On that beautiful, sunny day in Ireland, we really did have fun removing all the hair that I'd been so attached to.

When the last part of the hair had been shaved off with the beard trimmer, I needed a razor to take it right down to the skin. I wanted to see what I would look like being *completely* bald. I actually thought there was a chance I'd prefer it this way and never need to grow my hair back again! I wasn't sitting in front of a mirror while my head was being shaved, so I had no idea yet what I looked like. We'd all laughed so much during the shaving that when it was finally finished, I found myself in an ecstatic state of joy! Only then did I go to my own room to look at myself in the mirror.

That was a very strange experience. As I looked into the mirror, I realised the image I'd been so attached to was gone.

I felt my ego mind trying to reach out and grasp something from the reflection that no longer existed: I could no longer get false reassurance from seeing an image I'd created about myself. It was like I'd been getting a fix, just like from a drug, from viewing myself in a certain way, a way I thought I *needed* to be in order to feel safe.

Now what I saw was a reflection that I didn't identify with. In my perception, I didn't look either male or female. I didn't particularly like what I saw, but in that moment, I remembered the voice that reminded me I could deliberately choose joy. So, I decided to literally put a smile on my face and consciously choose to be joyful. In the instant I consciously chose joy, I felt a huge surge of elation fill my entire body and a warmth flood my heart that I'd never felt before. Something I'd been attached to left me in that moment, allowing something new and truly amazing to come into me. That former image I'd been so attached to had been a prison, and now I finally felt free!

I can't explain why, despite not really liking how I looked with no hair, I was perfectly okay with it. In fact, I felt immense happiness and amazingly light! I no longer cared what I looked like because the image I'd had of myself for so long was gone – it was a complete waste of time trying to get it back. I looked the way I did, and that was that.

I never thought it was possible to feel so free without liking what I saw in the mirror. It suddenly felt much easier for me to connect with others because I was no longer thinking about my appearance. I hadn't realised until then how much that obsession was running me; now, I just felt more relaxed around people. This seemed strange because all I'd ever wanted was to be loved and accepted by others, but I'd been carrying a misbelief that it'd come from how I looked. It seemed that now people found me more approachable, and they appeared to be much more relaxed around me, too.

It also became apparent over the next couple of days that most people who didn't know me assumed I had cancer. One man approached me at the airport telling me he knew what I was going through. I said it was very kind of him to share that with me but told him the real reason why I had no hair. He was extremely moved when he heard my story, and we made a wonderful connection. He then shared his own heartfelt journey with cancer. I felt honoured and humbled that he felt safe to share it with me. It was such a beautiful experience to be connecting with strangers so easily and on a deeper level.

It also felt like women, specifically, felt more comfortable being around me. The energy of comparison and competition so often present among women was no longer there, for me *or* for them. Perhaps it was the shift in my own energy that made them feel more at ease, as I was no longer focused on my own looks *or* theirs anymore. All I knew was that, yet again, human connection seemed easier and more free-flowing.

∼

I did decide to grow my hair back again, as I wanted to feel free from the obsession with appearance even when I had it. A deep shift had occurred in my being from the whole process of shaving my head. I discovered all my friends and family still loved me, even without my original look. My parents didn't fully understand why I needed to do something so drastic, and despite the fact they *really* disliked what I had done, I could tell they still loved and accepted me. It was only through actually receiving this unconditional love from them and others that I was fully able to believe I *was* lovable for more than just my appearance. In fact, I felt *more* love from others, not less, and my acceptance for myself grew tremendously.

When I released the belief that I was loved *only* because of the way I looked, and that it was just a lie I'd been telling myself anyway, I was indeed set free! Once I saw through the illusion my ego mind created, the Truth was experienced. When the Truth is revealed, it's *always* loving. And that is why:

Love is Truth and Love Will Set You Free!

Chapter 24

The Miracle Gift of Laughter

A ll my life, I longed to not care so much about what other people thought about me.

Consequently, I always tried to behave how others wanted me to. One message I received from my parents was not to be 'too much' of anything. If I laughed too loud, I was told to calm down. Too much joy made my parents uncomfortable, so I assumed everyone else in the world felt that way, too.

I learned very young to suppress my joy, but deep down, I envied people who could be playful and silly and not act so seriously all the time. They certainly seemed more relaxed and happier than me. It took over 40 years to discover the joy I'd suppressed in order to fit in.

～

In my forties, I was part of a spiritual community where we deliberately pushed ourselves to do things we'd always longed to do, despite the fear it elicited. We'd truly feel our feelings of fear and do it anyway. One day, I finally decided to face my resistance to being more carefree and playful. I had no idea what a transformation would occur and how it was going to change my life. The gifts were more lasting and profound than I could have imagined!

It happened when one of my friends in the group wanted someone to lead a laughter yoga session at her spiritual festival. She asked if I would take the training, as she thought I'd be really good at it. I thought she was joking. I didn't see what she obviously saw in me at the time.

The festival was three months away. The laughter yoga training course was taught over a weekend and cost around three hundred pounds. I was a bit miffed my friend didn't offer to pay for the course, considering I wasn't going to be paid for leading the session. This was one more reason I used to put it off, but really, I was doubtful about whether I was even capable to lead such a class.

One week before the laughter yoga training weekend was going to start in London, my friend called me again to see if I'd booked on the course. I finally agreed and called the woman leading the course. She told me it had been fully booked for months and that she only held two training weekends a year. My heart sank as I realised I'd lost my chance. That wasn't the reaction I'd expected! I thought I'd feel relieved and just accept it wasn't meant to be. Then she said, 'Oh, wait a minute! My colleague just told me one person dropped out! But if you'd like to join, I need payment today.' I was delighted, knowing at that moment I was definitely meant to be taking this course.

Laughter yoga involves no yoga poses whatsoever; it's simply people getting together to become more childlike and playful and to create spontaneous laughter. Yoga means unity, and when you laugh together for a long period of time, the joy created causes you to bond with everyone participating. In fact, it's said that nothing joins us quicker than when we laugh together, because it's practically impossible to judge someone you're having fun with!

On the day of the course, I woke up excited but also apprehensive. When I arrived, there were fewer people on the course than I'd expected, which gave me some sense of relief and comfort. We were in a small room, not a huge hall like I'd pictured. Everyone was so welcoming and happy, which put me immediately at ease.

During the first session, I felt extremely self-conscious and was absolutely sure my level of discomfort was obvious to everyone else. Being asked to make a funny face I didn't feel like making felt excruciating. If I hadn't paid over three hundred pounds for the course, I'm pretty sure I would have walked out at the break. I felt a huge regret, thinking I'd completely wasted my money. I had no idea how I was going to get through the whole weekend without dying of embarrassment.

I was relieved when we stopped for a break. I went to the bathroom and, after washing my hands, one of the other women in the group came in. I was dreading going back for the next session and asked her if she thought I looked ridiculous. Her reply took me by surprise. She seemed completely uninterested in me and what I looked like, saying very quickly, 'No but do *I* look ridiculous?' I was a little disappointed that she hadn't even noticed me; I couldn't understand how she could have missed how awkward and ridiculous I looked. I was baffled, and yet a very small part of me was also a little relieved that she hadn't noticed my discomfort.

I walked slowly back into the room, and we gathered in a circle for the next session. I was a tiny bit less anxious after the conversation with the woman in the bathroom, but still dreading what was coming. The facilitator said 'If any of you are feeling uncomfortable and even feeling a bit ridiculous, remember no one gives a damn about what you look like, because everyone else is only concerned about themselves.'

Bam! It was like a switch went off in my head. I felt the truth of her words go so deep within me that something changed. In that moment, I made a new choice, deciding I was going to stop worrying about what people thought of me and just start enjoying every minute of the course. It was a profound shift. I became a different person from that moment onwards.

I'm now able to catch the voice in my head that tells me not to do something I really want to do, just in case I might look silly or make a mistake. My mind loves to tell me, *If you do this, you're going to die.* When this happens now (which isn't very often), I simply say back, *Yeah, sure,* because I know it's clearly such a lie! I don't know *anyone* who has ever actually died of embarrassment, and yet the ego voice loves to tell me this, which stops me from fully living. I celebrate that now I'm usually the first to join in any fun on offer. I can get on the floor with children and be playful and free. I *love* to be silly, which was a real no-no when I was growing up.

The word 'silly' comes from the Middle English *seil*, or *seely*; from Old English *gasaelig*, meaning 'happy, fortuitous and prosperous'; and also from the German word *selig*, meaning 'blessed, happy and blissful'. Children were originally called these words because they played freely with no inhibitions. In their innocence, they were considered blessed. Over the years, the meaning 'blessed' in this context of play was changed to mean something derogative – the word 'silly', which we now view as negative. In fact, one dictionary definition of 'silly' says the following:

1. Having or exhibiting a lack of good judgement or common sense; foolishness.
2. Lacking seriousness or responsibleness; frivolous.
3. Semi-conscious, dazed.

What a complete change in meaning! I have to say, I'm *proud* to be able to call myself silly! I experience so much freedom in just having fun. I've danced through towns and streets with a group of friends wearing a clown's nose, and then (to *really* face my fears) done it by myself! I've worn a clown's nose in airports when travelling abroad and brought so much fun to others by doing so. Children love it, and the smiles just go on and on.

Truly, I've been blessed with the Truth and Love of laughter, joy and silliness, and:

The Truth Has Set Me Free!

Some findings about laughter:

- Laughter joins people together faster than anything else!
- A smile is a universal expression of happiness recognised by all cultures.
- Smiling and laughter are natural expressions; even babies that are born deaf and blind smile a lot!
- Small children laugh *400 times a day* on average; adults, only about 14.
- Fake smiling and laughter can also make us feel better, since the brain doesn't know the difference.
- Young people smile more frequently than older people.
- Women smile more often than men.
- Males with high testosterone levels smile the least of all.
- Laughter can be as healthy as physical exercise. Even older people and the less physically able can do it!
- Clapping stimulates endorphins.
- If you start the day with a smile before you get out of bed, you'll have a better day.

How laughter benefits the mind:

- Improves mental health
- Boosts creativity
- Reduces inhibitions
- Encourages openness, honesty, and a willingness to join others
- Encourages relief from guilt, trauma and future worries
- Keeps us in the present moment

How laughter benefits emotions:

- Reduces feelings of loneliness
- Improves empathy
- Restores hope
- Reinforces positive thinking
- Enhances generosity, communication, patience, trust, gratitude, inner peace, playfulness, honesty and emotional intelligence
- Promotes emotional maturity

How laughter benefits communities and workplaces:

- Increases attention span
- Enhances learning
- Fosters optimism
- More achieved with a positive attitude
- Increases creativity

- Improves self-confidence and self-esteem
- Boosts sense of security
- Improves leadership skills
- Improves team building
- Less fatigue, more energy and less absences, which leads to increased performance, added revenue and more positive results
- Reduces anger and increases happiness

How laughter benefits the body:

- Tones muscles for a natural facelift
- People who smile and laugh look more attractive to others
- Happy people are less ill
- Boosts production of hormones, endorphins, and serotonin, making it the best medicine for depression
- Kills pain
- Reduces blood pressure
- Improves cardiovascular system
- Enhances digestion
- Reduces insomnia
- Helps combat upper respiratory infections, as it increases oxygen intake to fight disease
- Less headaches, colds and flu
- Relaxes the body
- Reduces stress
- Boosts immune system by 40 percent

Chapter 25

Final Thoughts

What if our ultimate purpose here on earth is to discover that God, you, me and everything outside of us is *all* made of Love? That we are here to reconnect to that Love (even though most of the time we're not feeling that loving essence within ourselves or coming from others)?

Being born in the image and likeness of God refers to God's essence, which is pure Love; therefore, it's *our* true essence, too. We've forgotten this. We've become identified with our fearful, judging mind, which we call ego. This identification with ego creates an *illusion* of fear and separation from one another. But no matter what we've identified with, it will never change the fact that our pure essence *is* unconditional Love!

What if our only 'mistake', or original 'sin', was judging others and ourselves badly? What if we only did this because we felt so disconnected from our true nature? We can compare it to being like a programmed computer: Whatever we feed *into* a computer is what comes out of it, and just like a computer chip, our belief systems require a new chip. We need to feed ourselves with new information and then *live* by our new Knowledge – in this case, knowing we *are* pure, unadulterated Love.

When we act from Love and fully integrate it, it *will* become our new reality. Knowledge alone is not enough: We must create Love in action. I've come to understand this is what is meant by the Divine Feminine. The Divine Feminine (in both women *and* men) *is* Love in action! The Divine Masculine, on the other hand, is that which is unchangeable ... which is the fact that we *are* unconditional Love at our core. It's true the Divine Feminine is being birthed right now on this planet earth, as more and more beings identify with their true essence, becoming Love in action (instead of ego in action).

Imagine if we could put on a pair of glasses that enabled us to see past *all* our negative patterns and behaviours. All we'd see is beauty, innocence and Love radiating from everyone! Then we could discover those who behave the most unloving are, in fact, the ones most lost and disconnected from who they truly are. These are the ones who need to be loved into Wholeness. What if our mission is to seek Love's way, *not* judgement's way? What if *this* is what Jesus stood for when he stood for Truth? And what if this is what He meant when He said, 'You will do as I do and more'?

The ego mind tells us to fight for what we want, to use force and push against what we *think* we don't want. Love uses a power beyond the thinking mind. It uses the power of attraction, rather than egoic force, and by its action, it births wonderful new realities for those who embrace it! Love melts fear and hardness from around the hearts of those who truly feel its presence. This is precisely how heaven *can* exist on earth.

It's time to stop trying to heal others and trying to change what we see as wrong in the world and, instead, put all our focus and energy on changing our *own* beliefs and hearts. When we look through the eyes of innocence and see that *everyone's* true essence is Love, others *will* feel that perception we hold of them, and they'll be uplifted. After all, we can feel the effects of negative judgements from others; doesn't it make sense they can also feel our judgements upon them? When we judge someone, we actually help them stay the way they are. And if we get truly honest, who has *ever* responded well to our judgement? When has anyone (including ourselves) ever said, *Thank you very much for judging me. Now I'll go ahead and change?*

When we choose Love and forgiveness, we help people break old patterns. The same thing applies to when we judge ourselves unkindly. When we become aware of negative self-talk, we'll often notice we say things to ourselves that we would never dream of saying to someone else! When we do this, it just keeps us feeling badly, and our negative patterns continue.

I've learnt that each of our journeys to return to knowing our true essence is unique. Some will resonate with our journey home, and some will choose another path. It's essential that we honour each person's journey home to Love. This *will* unite us! It'll bring us together in harmony instead of creating different belief systems that fight against one another, declaring that our way is the 'right' way and other ways are 'wrong'. When we drop this mentality, we can learn from one another instead of fighting with one another.

Let's embrace everyone as equal. Let's embrace the knowledge that God loves each and every one of us equally no matter what we've temporarily forgotten. Then, we'll not reap the consequences of our actions from forgetting who we really are. Let's stop striving to be someone that stands out for achievements and accolades. Instead, let's become someone who's so content with knowing who we are that our Love touches and uplifts *everyone* we meet. We can be someone who radiates the Love we are through our thoughts, words, actions and being the presence of LOVE!

I've learnt on this journey that most of us are searching for happiness in a short-lived sort of way, leaving us feeling like there's still something missing even once we've reached our goals. Our 'completion' can't come from another human being, earning a lot of money or achieving something spectacular (like becoming a World Powerlifting Champion).

My own journey taught me that my power doesn't come from how strong I am physically, nor how successful I may be at a sport I love. It doesn't come from winning approval from others, either for my accomplishments or for my looks. It doesn't come from male respect, my father's or my partner's. It doesn't come from praise or attention from others, no matter how temporarily flattered I may feel. I once thought powerlifting would give me happiness, supplying all these things ... but it didn't.

I found my real power and strength from going within. Learning to listen to the gem of Love that lies in my own Heart is now my one true purpose. My journey continues as I learn every day how to better feel, think and act from the Love that lies within my own Heart. For me, Love *is* an action, not just a feeling. Now I know who I am, where I come from and where I'm going ... Ever deeper into the Love I was made to be.

For I've discovered the Truth: Love *is* what sets me free!

The poem below, entitled 'Love', I consider to be a powerful love prayer. As I wrote it, I truly felt it was coming from God/Universal Love. The words help me to know that I am here to love and be loved. My hope is that it may help you to know this, too.

Love

Cover me, enfold me, encase me in your Love.
Embrace me, release me, to fly just like a dove.

Free me, be me, take all of me and dance.
Remind me I am loved, God, to remove me from
    this trance.

I'm here to serve, please use me, in any way for
    Love.
And in my giving, I just know the angels smile
    above.

Radiate your Love, God, so I can clearly see
that only when I Love Love, then I will be free.

To Love myself, to be myself, to use the gift of time.
And only when I know I'm loved, will your heart
*   reach mine.*

Chapter 26

Simple (Yet Powerful!) Life-Changing Practices

These practices offer an opportunity to bring you more peace and connect you to the Love I've described throughout this book ... The Love that is your Divine Essence, which holds infinite wisdom and power to create miracles in your life.

When done consistently, over time, these very simple yet powerful practices *will* bring you more peace. They have profoundly improved my own wellbeing, and I continue them today.

1. Look for the beauty in everything.
2. Practise repeating the words 'Thank you for my life' in your mind throughout the day (especially first thing in the morning upon awakening, when the mind often searches for things to worry about!). It's important to remind ourselves to be grateful for all we *do* have.

3. Connect to your breath. Take deep, slow breaths throughout the day, as this will connect you to your heart and calm your nervous system. The result is that you'll start to feel more peaceful and less reactive. A breath work practice of your choice for five to 15 minutes in the morning is a great way to start the day. YouTube has many demonstrations of simple breath work practices; I recommend the Ted Talk by Max Strom called 'Breathe to Heal': https://youtu.be/4Lb5L-VEm34?si=A8wnVjw_EwD5xx8N (Hint: Putting a smile on your face while practising breath work can also help you become more joyful and less serious!)

4. Silently repeat the words 'I love you', followed by your name, as often as possible throughout the day and especially before you go to sleep at night. While repeating these words, say it from your heart as if it's coming directly from the Divine Universal Love that's created you and loves you unconditionally. This can be extremely powerful if you suffer from anxiety or depression. Keep in mind that the less you love and accept yourself right now, the more awkward this practice may feel at first, but it *will* get easier the more you continue the practice. So, feel the resistance and do it anyway. Don't allow the mind to doubt the process before even trying it for a few weeks. I had a bout of extreme depression after a relationship break up and this really did work for me. I now do it as an everyday practice.

You don't have to wait until your life is falling apart to start doing one (or all!) of these practices regularly. No matter where you are on your life's journey, these practices have the potential to connect you to the Love that *is* your Essence. When you connect to this Love more consciously, your vibration shifts, and you'll begin to notice you *can* deal with what life brings you in a much more calm and loving way. From my own experience, life still brings me challenges that help me grow, but many of the things I once saw as 'problems' no longer disturb my peace. This is because Love has shown me them from a completely different perspective. Which is *how* Love *will* set you free!

If beginning all the above practices at once seems overwhelming, you can start by choosing just one. At the end of the day, if you find that you only remembered the practice(s) once or twice, don't give up–this is quite normal! Eventually, they *will* come to you more naturally. I used to write the words 'Thank You' and 'I Love You' on the back of my hand to remind me!

Love in Action

Most importantly: Follow your joy! If you find yourself doing things because you think you 'should', but they don't make your heart sing, question your motives. Much of the time, we do things to please others due to unconscious fears that need to be realised and questioned.

Find reasons to celebrate yourself and your life. We *are* meant to be happy, yet so many people feel guilty just for enjoying themselves. Not doing what genuinely brings you joy creates a block to the Divine connection of your Soul calling. Your joy is your compass to living your true purpose. If the thought of doing something brings you joy, then find a way to do it *before* your ego mind talks you out of it.

Practice smiling at strangers. You can change someone's day just by giving them a smile! And of course, *you* will feel better by smiling more.

In conversations, be genuinely more interested in others rather than trying to 'sell' yourself to them. Find ways to uplift others and be as present as possible with whomever you find yourself speaking to. *You'll* start to feel uplifted because as you give to others, you give to yourself. Love is like a boomerang; it always comes back to you!

Chapter 27

My Future Vision

My desire is to create a community where people can come and be loved into Wholeness.

I truly believe humanity is desperate for connection. There are so many lonely people in the world today: homeless people, and people addicted to alcohol, drugs, internet, phones, shopping, food, pornography, unhealthy relationships, and more. A fantastic Ted Talk by Johann Hari called 'Everything You Think You Know About Addiction is Wrong' shows how the main cause of addiction and unhappiness *is* lack of connection: https://www.youtube.com/watch?v=PY9DcIMGxMs

The community I desire to create would be a nonprofit entity where people can come be with others and learn about the power of Universal Divine Love that is in each and every one of us. Once we connect to that Love, loneliness disappears. It will be a place to learn the power of breath, laughter therapy and self-inquiry to overcome fears.

Together, we'll learn to love and accept ourselves *and* learn about how important it is to extend that love to others.

This will be a place where food can be shared together for free or with donation, and unconditional love given to all. A place where people are fully accepted and treated as equals. A place where people can share their experiences, troubles or triumphs if they wish to, and where these sharings can then help others. A place where people are invited to give talks and workshops for free to help bring people together.

I genuinely believe these types of communities will open up all over the country once the benefits of them are proven, and perhaps will even spread throughout the world.

If you feel inspired to co-create this vision with me, please contact me via: www.lovetheultimtefreedom.com

Thank you!

Recommended Resources

Love Without Conditions by Paul Ferrini

Love Without End by Glenda Green

How Your Mind Can Heal Your Body by David Hamilton

A Course in Miracles by Jeshua, as channelled through Helen Schucman
acim.org

Way of Mastery by Jeshua, as channelled through Jayem
wayofmastery.com

The Afterlife of Billy Fingers by Annie Kagan

Loving What Is by Byron Katie

Conversations With God by Neil Donald Walsch

The Little Soul and The Sun by Neil Donald Walsch

Support for Addictions *

Alcoholics Anonymous (alcohol addiction)
www.aa.org

Al-Anon (support for friends and family of
alcoholics)
www.al-anon.org

Adult Children of Alcoholics & Dysfunctional
Families
www.adultchildren.org

Cocaine Anonymous
www.ca.org

Coda (co-dependency addiction)
www.coda.org

Gamblers Anonymous
www.gamblersanonymous.org

Sex and Love Addicts Anonymous (S.L.A.A.)
www.slaafws.org

* There are many more Twelve Step programs for various addictions than are listed here. I recommend utilising online searches to find local support groups.

Acknowledgments

Firstly, I would like to express my deepest gratitude for Jacalyn Hunt who supported and encouraged me to write this book. Her belief in me, and that my experiences could help many people, inspired me to do so. Without her continued help, time and experience during the first year of me writing down my experiences this book would not be in your hands.

I would also like to thank all my friends that took me into their homes and gave me a place to stay: From the US, John Mark and Cindy Stroud, Bernadette Eden, Cori Russell, Gail Leopold, Laura Herbert and Marianne 'O Sheeran. From the UK: Michael Foster, Wendy Thacker, Kerry Sophia Davis, Ian Green and my Uncle Richard and Aunty Anne. From Holland, Ori Ana Lightning.

Thank you to Sandy Levy-Lundén for her process The Power of Clearing (*www.sandylevey.com*) and to Byron Katie (*thework.com*) for The Work, both of which profoundly impacted my journey of awakening.

A huge thank you for the wisdom and guidance of Jayem, who channelled *The Way of Mastery*, for showing me the importance of connecting with the breath and recognising the ego to overcome my fears. (*wayofmastery.com*)

Thank you to John Mark Stroud for encouraging me to trust the silent voice within me and giving me the courage to share the messages I receive with others on a one-to-one basis via channelling. (*onewhowakes.org*)

To Ori Ana Lightning for also encouraging me and trusting the channelled messages I bring through, and for his dedication to sound healing and bringing through the healing tones for singing the Lord's Prayer in Aramaic. (*dragonhearttemple.com*)

To all the friends on my journey who have shown me so much love and support: All the already mentioned above and Steve Corwin (US), Moira Snape (UK), Peter and Lynn McIntosh (Pyramids of Chi, Bali), and Annette Campbell (US).

To my copyeditor and proof reader Dawn Hammer. (*hammerproofreading.com*)

And to Danielle and the team at Wrate's Editing Services for designing the front cover and helping me with formatting and self-publishing on Amazon. (*wrateseditingservices.co.uk*)

Thank you!

About the Author

For the first 30 years of her life, Rosie-Maria Love, who grew up in the UK, focused on excelling in two international sports: springboard diving and powerlifting (she became a World Powerlifting champion). Now, instead of seeking to have a powerful body, she chooses to practice the power of Love.

Rosie-Maria hit rock bottom when she fell in love with an alcoholic. Realizing she couldn't change him, she wanted to end her own life. This led her to discover and examine her co-dependency – needing things outside of herself to be a certain way *so* she could be happy.

For the last 24 years, Rosie-Maria's journey has taken her on a path to seek the Truth that will set her free. Through dedication and commitment to that Truth, she's experienced many wonderful, life-changing transformations.

Rosie-Maria is an international workshop facilitator, taking clients on deep journeys into releasing the blocks that prevent them from knowing themselves *as* Love. Her one-on-one sessions help many beings find more Love and peace. She's a qualified Power of Clearing coach, breathwork coach, Laughter Healing coach ... and has an amazing singing voice! She's well-known for bringing powerful healing tones through her voice when singing *The Lord's Prayer* in Aramaic. Singing this powerful prayer brings her into a state of perfect presence where she's able to access what's been described to her as the One Mind of Truth, a Truth that is True always: Love. This One Mind is our Highest Selves, the God essence within us all that knows only Love is Real. (To hear Rosie-Maria sing the powerful Aramaic *Lord's Prayer*, please visit this link: https://youtu.be/aCAS31M7mlA)

Testimonials

'Rosie-Maria, that was the retreat to end all retreats! Mind-blowing, heart-opening. Thank you!' *Pam*

'A Dynamite workshop. It blasted a lot of old stuff out! Wow! Rosie-Maria, you are a dear gift from Divine Mother, a light on our path!' *Anne K*

'Wow, soft power streaming forth from the wisdom being shared through this, our beautiful Sister, known to me as Rosie-Maria Love. Tears pouring down my cheeks at the recognition of being in the presence of pure unconditional Love without it being fluffy ... I encourage anyone to ask for a private channelling through Rosie-Maria. They have assisted me so much on my Awakening journey'! *Ori Ana Lightning*

You may contact Rosie-Maria at:
rosiemaria@lovetheultimatefreedom.com

Printed in Great Britain
by Amazon